AIR FRYER COOKBOOK

5-Ingredient Recipes for Endless Flavors and Affordable Cooking

Alisha Mills

Warning-Disclaimer

The purpose of this book is to educate and entertain. The author or publisher does not guarantee that anyone following the techniques, suggestions, tips, ideas, or strategies will become successful. The author and publisher shall have neither liability or responsibility to anyone with respect to any loss or damage caused, or alleged to be caused, directly or indirectly by the information contained in this book.

CONTENTS

SNACKS AND APPETIZERS 25

POULTRY RECIPES 41

FISH AND SEAFOOD 58

VEGETABLES AND SIDES 83

SWEETS 99

INTRODUCTION

Hello and welcome to a culinary adventure – "Air Fryer Cookbook: 5 Ingredients." Unlock the secrets of effortless cooking with just a handful of simple ingredients.

In this cookbook, we've curated a collection of irresistible recipes to elevate your air frying experience. Each dish is a masterpiece of flavor and simplicity, from crispy appetizers to succulent mains and indulgent desserts.

Say goodbye to kitchen chaos and hello to culinary bliss as you discover the magic of air frying. With easy-to-follow instructions and stunning photography to inspire your inner chef, preparing delicious meals has never been easier.

Prepare to revolutionize your cooking routine and delight your taste buds with every bite. Welcome to a world of flavor, welcome to "Air Fryer Cookbook: 5 Ingredients."

HOW DOES THE AIR FRYER WORK?

Using an air fryer for baking or cooking is straightforward. Contrary to what you might think, air fryers don't fry food. They operate by circulating hot air using a heating element and fan, with an exhaust outlet to manage temperature and remove excess heat.

Air fryers are equipped with precise controls for time and temperature, ensuring optimal cooking results. You can tailor these settings for different types of food and ingredients. Typically, foods in an air fryer are cooked between 150°C and 200°C, taking about 8 to 25 minutes, often requiring a light oil coating for that crispy, golden finish.

Remember, air fryers are electric appliances that need a power source. They come with baskets or pans for placing the food, and for even cooking, it's advisable to shake or toss the contents occasionally.

ADVANTAGE OF AIR FRYER

Air fryers have become a revolutionary tool in kitchen and meal preparation. But what does this mean for you, the everyday user? Here's a look at some key advantages you can enjoy by incorporating an air fryer into your cooking routine.

- **Health Benefits:** The most significant advantage of an air fryer is its contribution to better health. By using significantly less oil than traditional deep frying, meals prepared in air fryers have reduced fat content. This decrease in oil usage can lower the risk of cholesterol issues, heart diseases, and inflammation. Additionally, reducing unhealthy oil and calories can prevent unwanted weight gain.

- **Time:** Efficiency Although the size of air fryers may necessitate cooking in batches, they offer a time-saving benefit. Air fryers typically cook food within 8 to 25 minutes, delivering crispy and delicious results.

Compared with other frying methods, air fryers provide a quicker and equally satisfying cooking experience, making them a valuable kitchen investment.

- *Safety:* Air fryers offer a safer cooking environment, eliminating concerns about oil spills and splashes. Adhering to the manufacturer's guidelines can avoid common kitchen accidents like burns, scalds, and fires. This makes air fryers safer, especially for households with children or those new to cooking.

MISTAKES TO AVOID WHEN USING AN AIR FRYER

Air fryer users often make mistakes that can harm their appliances or result in subpar meals. Below are some frequent errors and tips on how to avoid them.

- **Excessive Oil Use:** Your air fryer only needs two teaspoons or a light oil coating. Overusing oil can lead to undercooked meals.

- **Cooking Damp Food:** Air fryers are not designed to remove moisture, so avoid putting in wet food as it can damage the appliance. Stick to dry, crunchy, or breaded items.

- **Crowding the Air Fryer:** Ensure ample space around your air fryer for efficient operation and proper ventilation.

- **Cooking Tiny Food Items:** Be cautious with food items, as they can fall through the basket or pan and burn, causing smoke.

- **Neglecting to Clean:** Regular cleaning of your air fryer is essential, even if it doesn't appear dirty. Use warm water and dish soap after each use.

- **Overfilling:** Resist the temptation to overload your air fryer. Cook in batches for even heat distribution and better cooking results.

TIPS AND TRICKS FOR OPTIMAL AIR FRYER USAGE

To get the most out of your air fryer and maintain it properly, here are some simple yet effective tips:

1. Thoroughly read the owner's manual before the first use.
2. Allow the air fryer to cool before cleaning or storing it.
3. Wipe the exterior with a damp cloth and clean the interior with a sponge in hot water.
4. Wash pans, baskets, and removable parts with dish soap and hot water. These parts are generally dishwasher safe, but ensure they are dry before reassembling.
5. Use rubber-tipped tongs instead of metal ones to prevent scratching.
6. For stuck-on food, soak the pan or basket in soapy hot water for easy removal.
7. Regularly inspect plugs and cords for cleanliness and damage.
8. In case of smoke, turn off the appliance and remove any fallen food items or grease.
9. To eliminate odors, clean the basket or pan with soap and water, and use lemon juice for persistent smells. Rewash to remove the lemon scent.

WHY A 5-INGREDIENT AIR FRYER COOKBOOK

In my approach to a 5-ingredient air fryer cookbook, **I don't count staple items like salt, pepper, oil, and sugar as part of the main ingredients. These are considered basic pantry essentials that most people already have in their kitchen.**

I focus on the five main ingredients that define each recipe, assuming that these everyday items are readily available for general use.This method allows me to keep the recipes simple and accessible yet flexible enough to enhance flavors using these everyday staples.

Simplicity and Convenience

With only five ingredients per recipe, these cookbooks make cooking less daunting, especially for beginners or those with a busy lifestyle. The simplicity allows for quick understanding and preparation of meals, making cooking more approachable and less time-consuming.

Cost-Effective

Using fewer ingredients can significantly reduce your grocery bill. It encourages you to buy less and make the most of what you already have in your pantry, leading to less waste and more economical meal planning.

Creativity and Innovation

Working with a limited number of ingredients can spark creativity in the kitchen. It challenges you to think differently about flavor combinations and cooking techniques, leading to unique and innovative dishes.

Focus on Quality

With fewer ingredients, there's a greater focus on the quality of each component. This encourages the use of fresh, high-quality ingredients that can make a significant difference in the flavor and overall quality of your meals.

Healthier Eating

5-ingredient recipes often rely on whole, unprocessed foods, which can contribute to a healthier diet. The simplicity of the ingredients list makes it easier to control what goes into your food, helping you avoid unwanted additives and preservatives commonly found in more complex recipes or processed foods.

HAPPY COOKING!

BREAKFAST AND LUNCH

Bacon, Tomato, Egg, and Bean Breakfast

Serves: 2 | Total Time: 30 minutes

INGREDIENTS

1 tbsp melted butter
200g cooked white beans
2 tomatoes, halved

Salt and black pepper to taste
6 bacon strips
2 eggs

DIRECTIONS

Preheat your Air Fryer to 180°C. Season the tomato slices with salt and black pepper. Lightly grease a ramekin with melted butter. Crack in the eggs. Place the ramekin with the cracked eggs in the air fryer basket alongside the bacon and tomatoes. Cook for 8-10 minutes, flipping the bacon halfway through, until the bacon is crispy and the tomatoes are tender. Pour the cooked beans into a separate ramekin.

When the air fryer beeps, remove the eggs, tomatoes, and bacon from the air fryer basket. Place the ramekin with the beans into the air fryer basket. Cook for an addi tional 5 minutes. Carefully remove everything from the air fryer basket and divide onto plates. Serve and enjoy!

Pepperoni English Muffin Sandwiches

Serves: 4 | Total Time: 25 minutes

INGREDIENTS

4 muffins
8 pepperoni slices

4 cheddar cheese slices
1 tomato, sliced

DIRECTIONS

Preheat your Air Fryer to 180°C. Split the English muffins along the crease. Layer 2 slices of pepperoni, a slice of cheese, and a slice of tomato on the bottom half of each muffin. Place the top half to complete the sandwiches. Lightly spray with cooking oil. Place the muffin sandwiches in the air fryer. Bake for 8 minutes, flipping once. Let stand for 10 minutes before serving.

Cheese and Bacon Egg Muffins

Serves 6 | Total Time: 30 minutes

INGREDIENTS

3 eggs
2 tbsp double cream
¼ tsp Dijon mustard

Salt and black pepper to taste
100g cooked bacon, crumbled
30g grated cheddar

DIRECTIONS

Preheat your Air Fryer to 170°C. Beat the eggs with salt and pepper in a bowl until fluffy. Stir in the double cream, mustard, cooked bacon, and cheese. Divide the mixture between 6 greased muffin cups and place them in the frying basket. Bake for 8-10 minutes. Let cool slightly before serving.

Kale and Mushrooms Egg Cups

Serves: 6 | Total Time: 20 minutes

INGREDIENTS

250g white mushrooms, sliced
6 eggs, beaten
Salt and black pepper to taste

½ tsp chilli powder
120g kale, chopped
2 green onions, diced

DIRECTIONS

Preheat your Air Fryer to 180°C. In a large mixing bowl, combine the beaten eggs, salt, black pepper, and chili powder. Whisk until well combined. Fold in the mushrooms, kale, diced green onions.

Spoon the mixture evenly into 6 greased muffin cups, filling each cup about three-quarters full. Place the filled muffin cups into the Air Fryer basket.

Bake the egg muffins in the Air Fryer for 12-15 minutes, or until the muffins are puffed up, set, and lightly golden on top. Carefully remove the egg muffins from the Air Fryer and allow them to cool for a few minutes before serving. Enjoy!

Honey Cereal Bread Sticks

Serves: 3 | Total Time: 20 minutes

INGREDIENTS

4 sandwich bread slices
2 eggs, beaten
50ml milk

150g crushed sweet cereals
30ml honey

DIRECTIONS

Preheat your Air Fryer to 185°C. Slice the bread into sticks. Whisk the eggs and milk in a bowl. Put the cereals on a plate. Submerge the sticks into the egg mixture, then coat them in the fruity pebbles. Place the breadsticks in the greased frying basket and Air Fry for 5-6 minutes, flipping once. Serve immediately with honey as a dip.

Cinnamon Apple French Toast

Serves: 1 | Total Time: 30 minutes

INGREDIENTS

2 white bread slices
2 eggs
½ peeled apple, sliced

1 tbsp cinnamon sugar
50g whipped cream

DIRECTIONS

Preheat your Air Fryer to 180°C. Whisk eggs and cinnamon sugar until fluffy. Dip bread slices in the egg mixture, then place in the greased Air Fryer basket. Top with apple slices.

Air Fry for 20 minutes, flipping halfway through, until bread is nicely browned and apples are crispy. Place one bread slice on a plate, spread whipped cream evenly, top with caramelized apple slices, and cover with the second bread slice. Serve immediately.

Apple Peanut Butter Energy Bites

Serves: 6 | Total Time: 15 minutes

INGREDIENTS

1 apple, grated
150g oat flour
2 tbsp honey

40g peanut butter
50g raisins

DIRECTIONS

Preheat your Air Fryer to 180°C. In a bowl, combine the diced apple, flour, honey, peanut butter, and raisins. Mix until well combined.

Roll the mixture into balls. Place them onto parchment paper and flatten them slightly. Place the flattened balls into the Air Fryer and Bake for 9-10 minutes, or until slightly brown. Enjoy!

Berry Dutch Pannenkoek

Serves: 4 | Total Time: 30 minutes

INGREDIENTS

3 eggs, beaten
75g buckwheat flour
75ml milk

200g berries, crushed
2 tbsp icing sugar

DIRECTIONS

Preheat your Air Fryer to 170°C.

In a mixing bowl, whisk together the eggs, buckwheat flour, and milk until smooth. Pour the pancake batter into a greased baking pan. Place the baking pan into the preheated Air Fryer.

Bake for 12-16 minutes or until the pancake is puffed and golden brown. Carefully remove the baking pan from the Air Fryer. Using a spatula, gently flip the Dutch pancake over onto a plate. Sprinkle the cooked pancake with fresh berries and dust with icing sugar. Enjoy!

Gammon and Cheese Sandwiches

Serves: 2 | Total Time: 15 minutes

INGREDIENTS

1 tsp olive oil
4 bread slices
4 gammon slices

4 Cheddar cheese slices
4 thick tomato slices
1 tsp dried oregano

DIRECTIONS

Preheat your Air Fryer to 180°C. Drizzle olive oil and sprinkle oregano on one side of each bread slice. On one of the slices (with the unoiled side facing up), layer 2 slices of gammon ham, 2 slices of cheese, and 2 slices of tomato. Place the unoiled side of another piece of bread on top, creating a sandwich.

Place the sandwiches in the Air Fryer basket with the oiled side down. Bake for 8 minutes, flipping once halfway through. Let the sandwiches cool slightly, then cut them in half and serve.

Salmon and Cheese Quiche

Serves: 4 | Total Time: 30 minutes

INGREDIENTS

100g shredded Gruyere cheese
1 refrigerated pie crust
2 eggs

50ml milk
Salt and black pepper to taste
150g cooked salmon

DIRECTIONS

Preheat your Air Fryer to 180°C. Add the crust to a baking dish and press it firmly. Trim off any excess edges. Poke a few holes in the crust with a fork. In a bowl, beat the eggs. Stir in the milk, salmon, half of the cheese, salt, and pepper. Mix well, breaking the salmon into chunks and ensuring it's evenly distributed among the other ingredients. Transfer the mix to the baking dish.

Place the baking dish in the Air Fryer and Bake for 15 minutes until the quiche is firm and almost crusty. Slide the basket out and top with the remaining cheese. Cook further for 5 minutes or until golden brown. Let cool slightly and serve.

Delicious Morning Sausage Bites

Serves: 4 | Total Time: 25 minutes

INGREDIENTS

500g minced pork sausages
50g diced onions
¼ tsp ground nutmeg

½ tsp fennel
¼ tsp garlic powder
Salt and black pepper to taste

DIRECTIONS

Preheat your Air Fryer to 170°C. In a large mixing bowl, combine all ingredients. Take small portions of the mixture and roll them into balls using your hands. Place the meatballs in the greased Air Fryer basket, ensuring they are not overcrowded. Air Fry for 10-12 minutes, flipping once halfway through the cooking time, until the meatballs are cooked through and browned on the outside. Serve immediately.

Cheese and Bacon Sandwich

Serves: 1 | Total Time: 30 minutes

INGREDIENTS

1 muffin, halved
1 egg

1 slice bacon
1 slice provolone cheese

DIRECTIONS

Preheat your Air Fryer to 170°C. Put the muffin, crusty side up, in the frying basket. Place a slice of bacon next to the muffins and Bake for 5 minutes. Flip the bacon and muffins, and lay a slice of provolone cheese on top of the muffins. Beat the egg in a small heatproof bowl.

Add the bowl in the frying basket next to the bacon and muffin and Bake for 15 minutes, or until the cheese melts, bacon is crispy and eggs set. Remove the muffin to a plate, layer a slice of bacon, then the egg and top with the second toasted muffin.

Apricot Mini Pies

Serves: 6 | Total Time: 35 minutes

INGREDIENTS

2 refrigerated piecrusts
30g apricot jam
1 tsp cornflour

75g sweet vanilla yogurt
30g cream cheese

DIRECTIONS

Preheat your Air Fryer to 180°C. Lay out pie crusts on a flat surface. Cut each sheet of pie crust with a knife into three rectangles for a total of 6 rectangles. Mix apricot jam and cornflour in a small bowl. Cover the top half of one rectangle with 1 tbsp of the apricot mixture. Repeat for all rectangles. Fold the bottom of the crust over the preserve-covered top. Crimp and seal all edges with a fork.

Lightly coat each tart with cooking oil, then place it into the air fryer without stacking. Bake for 10 minutes. Prepare the frosting by mixing yogurt and cream cheese. When done, let the pies cool completely. Frost the pies. Serve.

Lorraine-Inspired Egg Cakes

Serves: 6 | Total Time: 30 minutes

INGREDIENTS

3 eggs, whisked
2 tbsp single cream
Salt and black pepper to taste

100g cooked bacon, crumbled
50g grated Swiss cheese
1 tomato, sliced

DIRECTIONS

Preheat your Air Fryer to 170°C. Mix the egg, single cream, salt, and black pepper in a bowl. Divide bacon and cheese between 6 lightly greased silicone cupcakes. Spread the egg mixture between cupcakes evenly. Top each with a tomato slice. Place them in the frying basket and Bake for 8-10 minutes. Serve hot.

Feta and Potato Bowls

Serves: 2 | Total Time: 25 minutes

INGREDIENTS

1 russet potato, cubed
1 pepper, cut into strips
70g feta, cubed

1 tbsp nutritional yeast
1 tbsp apple cider vinegar

DIRECTIONS

Preheat your Air Fryer to 200°C. Put the potato cubes and pepper strips in the Air Fryer basket and Air Fry for 10 minutes. In a small pan, combine feta cheese, nutritional yeast, and apple cider vinegar.

Fit a trivet in the Air Fryer and place the pan with the feta mixture on top. Air Fry for 5 minutes until the potatoes are tender and the feta cheese is cooked. Divide the cooked potatoes and peppers into 2 bowls. Top each bowl with the feta scramble. Serve immediately.

Breakfast Quesadillas with Bacon

Serves: 4 | Total Time: 30 minutes

INGREDIENTS

8 flour tortillas
200g cooked bacon, crumbled
6 eggs, scrambled

250g grated cheddar
1 tsp chopped chives
Black pepper to taste

DIRECTIONS

Preheat your Air Fryer to 170°C. Put 1 tortilla in the bottom of a cake pan. Spread ¼ portion of each crumbled bacon, eggs, chives, black pepper, and cheese over the tortilla and top with a second tortilla. Place the cake pan in the frying basket and Bake for 4 minutes. Set aside on a large plate and repeat the process with the remaining ingredients. Let cool for 3 minutes before slicing. Serve right away.

Scallion Egg Bites

Serves: 6 | Total Time: 35 minutes

INGREDIENTS

60g shredded Muenster cheese
5 eggs, beaten
3 tbsp sour cream

Salt and black pepper to taste
40g minced pepper
3 tbsp minced scallions

DIRECTIONS

Preheat your Air Fryer to 160°C. Make a foil sling: Fold a 40-cm-long piece of heavy-duty aluminum foil lengthwise into thirds. Combine the eggs, sour cream, salt, and pepper in a bowl. Add the peppers, scallions, and cheese and stir. Add the mixture to 6 egg bite cups, making sure to get some of the solids in each cup.

Put the egg bite pan on the sling you made and lower it into the fryer. Leave the foil in but bend down the edges, so they fit. Bake the bites for 10-15 minutes or until a toothpick inserted into the center comes out clean. Remove the egg bite pan using the foil sling. Cool for 5 minutes, then turn the pan upside down over a plate to remove the egg bites. Serve warm.

Cream Cheese and Chorizo Biscuits

Serves: 4 | Total Time: 20 minutes

INGREDIENTS

350g chorizo sausage
200g tinned biscuits

1 tbsp cream cheese

DIRECTIONS

Preheat your Air Fryer to 180°C. Shape the sausage into 4 patties. Bake in the air fryer for 10 minutes, turning once halfway through. Remove and set aside.

Separate the biscuit dough into 5 biscuits, then place in the air fryer for 5 minutes, flipping once. Remove from the air fryer. Divide each biscuit in half. Smear 1 tsp of cream cheese on the bottom half, top with the sausage, and then cover with the top half. Serve warm.

Parma Ham and Cheese Cakes

Serves: 4 | Total Time: 25 minutes

INGREDIENTS

4 crusty rolls
4 Gouda cheese thin slices
5 eggs

2 tbsp double cream
3 Parma ham slices, chopped
Salt and black pepper to taste

DIRECTIONS

Preheat your Air Fryer to 170°C. Slice off the top of the rolls, then tear out the insides with your fingers, leaving about 1-cm of bread to make a shell. Press one cheese slice inside the roll shell until it takes the shape of the roll.

Beat eggs with double cream in a medium bowl. Next, mix in the remaining ingredients. Spoon the egg mixture into the rolls lined with cheese. Place rolls in the greased frying basket and Bake until eggs are puffy and brown, 8-12 minutes. Serve the cakes warm.

Bacon Toasts

Serves: 4 | Total Time: 25 minutes

INGREDIENTS

4 French bread slices
2 tbsp olive oil
4 eggs
2 tbsp milk

Salt and black pepper to taste
120g cooked bacon, crumbled
90g grated Colby cheese

DIRECTIONS

Preheat your Air Fryer to 170°C. Drizzle each slice of bread with olive oil and Bake in the frying basket for 2-3 minutes until light brown; set aside. Beat together the eggs, milk, salt, and pepper in a bowl.

Transfer to a 15-cm cake pan and place the pan into the fryer. Bake for 7-8 minutes, stirring once or until the eggs are set. Transfer the egg mixture to a bowl. Top the bread slices with egg mixture, bacon, and cheese. Return to the fryer and Bake for 4-8 minutes or until the cheese melts and browns in spots.

Cheesy Scrambled Eggs

Serves 2 | Total Time: 15 minutes

INGREDIENTS

1 tbsp cottage cheese, crumbled
4 eggs
Salt and black pepper to taste

2 tsp double cream
1 tbsp chopped parsley

DIRECTIONS

Preheat your Air Fryer to 200°C. In a bowl, beat the eggs with salt and pepper. Pour the beaten eggs into a greased pan that fits inside your Air Fryer basket. Place the pan in the frying basket and Air Fry for 5 minutes. Using a silicone spatula, stir in the double cream, cottage cheese, and half of the parsley and Air Fry for another 2 minutes. Scatter with parsley to serve.

Turkey Patties

Serves 4 | Total Time: 30 minutes

INGREDIENTS

350g turkey sausage
1 tsp onion powder
1 tsp dried coriander

¼ tsp Thai curry paste
¼ tsp red pepper flakes
Salt and black pepper to taste

DIRECTIONS

Preheat your Air Fryer to 170°C. Put the sausage, onion, coriander, curry paste, red flakes, salt, and black pepper in a large bowl and mix well. Form into eight patties. Arrange the patties on the greased frying basket and Air Fry for 10 minutes, flipping once halfway through. Serve hot.

Cheesy Frittata with Pancetta

Serves 2 | Total Time: 25 minutes

INGREDIENTS

4 cooked pancetta slices, chopped
5 eggs
Salt and black pepper to taste

½ leek, thinly sliced
75g grated cheddar cheese
2 tbsp milk

DIRECTIONS

Preheat your Air Fryer to 160°C. Beat the eggs, milk, salt, and pepper in a bowl. Mix in pancetta and cheddar. Transfer to a greased with olive oil baking pan. Place it in the frying basket. Bake for 14 minutes. Let cool for 5 minutes. Serve and enjoy!

Apple and Cherry Oatmeal Cups

Serves: 2 | Total Time: 20 minutes

INGREDIENTS

1 cored apple, diced
4 pitted cherries, diced
100g rolled oats

½ tsp ground cinnamon
100ml milk

DIRECTIONS

Preheat your Air Fryer to 170°C. Mix the apple, cherries, oats, and cinnamon in a heatproof bowl. Add in milk and Bake for 6 minutes. Then, stir well and Bake for 6 more minutes until the fruit is soft. Serve.

Cinnamon Caramelized Peaches

Serves: 6 | Total Time: 25 minutes

INGREDIENTS

3 pitted peaches, halved
2 tbsp brown sugar
230ml double cream

¼ tsp ground cinnamon
170g fresh blueberries

DIRECTIONS

Preheat your Air Fryer to 190°C. Lay the peaches in the frying basket with the cut side up, then top them with brown sugar. Bake for 7-11 minutes, allowing the peaches to brown around the edges.

In a mixing bowl, whisk double cream, and cinnamon until stiff peaks form. Fold the peaches into a plate. Spoon the cream mixture into the peach cups, top with blueberries, and serve.

Vegetables with Gammon

Serves 4 | Total Time: 25 minutes

INGREDIENTS

25 Brussels sprouts, halved
2 mini sweet peppers, diced
1 yellow onion, diced

3 gammon slices, diced
2 tbsp orange juice
¼ tsp salt

DIRECTIONS

Preheat your Air Fryer to 170°C. Mix the sprouts, sweet peppers, onion, deli ham, orange juice, and salt in a bowl. Transfer to the frying basket and Air Fry for 12 minutes, tossing once. Serve.

Cheddar Brunch Burrito

Serves: 4 | Total Time: 15 minutes

INGREDIENTS

2 hard-boiled eggs, chopped
60g grated cheddar cheese
1 red pepper, chopped

3 tbsp salsa
4 flour tortillas

DIRECTIONS

Preheat your Air Fryer to 200°C. Combine the eggs, cheddar cheese, red pepper, and salsa in a bowl. Spoon the mixture into the tortillas. Fold the edges and roll up the tortillas to form burritos.

Secure each burrito with a toothpick to hold its shape. Place the prepared burritos in the Air Fryer frying basket. Air Fry for 3-5 minutes until the burritos are crispy and golden brown. Serve hot.

Chorizo and Cheese Balls

Serves 4 | Total Time: 25 minutes

INGREDIENTS

1 egg white
450g chorizo minced sausage
2 tbsp tinned green chiles

30g bread crumbs
30g grated cheddar cheese

DIRECTIONS

Preheat your Air Fryer to 200°C. Mix all ingredients in a large bowl. Form into 16 balls. Put the sausage balls in the frying basket and Air Fry for 6 minutes. When done, shake the basket and cook for an additional 6 minutes. Transfer to a serving plate and serve.

Easy Popovers

Serves 2 | Total Time: 30 minutes

INGREDIENTS

5 eggs
1 tbsp milk
2 tbsp double cream

Salt and black pepper to taste
⅛ tsp ground nutmeg
30g grated Swiss cheese

DIRECTIONS

Preheat your Air Fryer to 170°C. Beat all ingredients in a bowl. Divide between greased muffin cups and place them in the frying basket. Bake for 8-10 minutes. Cool slightly before serving.

Chicken Frittata Cakes

Serves 2 | Total Time: 30 minutes

INGREDIENTS

100g shredded cooked chicken breasts
3 eggs
2 tbsp double cream

4 tsp Tabasco sauce
60g grated Asiago cheese

DIRECTIONS

Preheat your Air Fryer to 170°C. Beat all ingredients in a bowl. Divide the egg mixture between greased 6 muffin cupcakes and place them in the frying basket. Bake for 8-10 minutes until set. Leave to cool slightly before serving the cakes.

Spiced Courgette Hash Browns

Serves: 4 | Total Time: 20 minutes

INGREDIENTS

2 shredded courgettes
2 tbsp nutritional yeast

1 tsp allspice
1 egg white

DIRECTIONS

Preheat your Air Fryer to 200°C.

In a bowl, combine courgettes, nutritional yeast, allspice, and egg white. Mix well to combine. Form the mixture into 4 patties. Cut 4 pieces of parchment paper, put a patty on each foil.

Fold in all sides to create a rectangle. Use a spatula to flatten and spread the patties evenly. Then unwrap each foil and remove the hash browns onto the fryer, and Air Fry for 12 minutes until golden brown and crispy, turning once. Serve right away.

SNACKS AND APPETIZERS

Speedy Beer-Battered Onion Rings

Serves: 4 | Total Time: 20 minutes

INGREDIENTS

2 sliced onions, rings separated
120g flour
Salt and pepper to taste

1 tsp garlic powder
240 ml beer

DIRECTIONS

Preheat your Air Fryer to 170°C. In a mixing bowl, combine the flour, garlic powder, beer, salt, and black pepper. Dip the onion rings into the bowl and lay the coated rings in the frying basket. Air Fry for 15 minutes, shaking the basket several times during cooking to jostle the onion rings and ensure a good, even fry. Once ready, the onions should be crispy and golden brown. Serve hot.

Cheesy Avocado Fries

Serves: 2 | Total Time: 20 minutes

INGREDIENTS

1 egg
2 tbsp milk
Salt and pepper to taste

120g crushed chilli corn chips
2 tbsp Parmesan cheese
1 avocado, sliced into fries

DIRECTIONS

Preheat your Air Fryer to 185°C. In a bowl, beat egg and milk. In another bowl, add crushed chips, Parmesan cheese, salt, and pepper. Dip avocado fries into the egg mixture, then dredge into the crushed chips mixture to coat. Place avocado fries in the greased frying basket and Air Fry for 5 minutes. Serve.

Tasty Potato Chips

Serves: 2 | Total Time: 30 minutes

INGREDIENTS

1 tsp dry ranch seasoning
Salt and pepper to taste
250g sliced potatoes

2 tsp olive oil
30ml white wine vinegar

DIRECTIONS

Preheat your Air Fryer to 200°C. In a bowl, combine ranch mix, salt, and pepper. Reserve ½ tsp for garnish. In another bowl, mix sliced fingerling potatoes with vinegar and stir around. Let soak in the vinegar water for at least thirty minutes, then drain them and pat them dry.

Place potato chips and spread with olive oil until coated. Sprinkle with the ranch mixture and toss to coat. Place potato chips in the frying basket and Air Fry for 16 minutes, shaking 4 times. Transfer it to a bowl. Sprinkle with the reserved mixture and let sit for 15 minutes. Serve immediately.

Hot Prawns

Serves: 4 | Total Time: 15 minutes

INGREDIENTS

450g prawns, cleaned and deveined
4 tbsp olive oil
½ lime, juiced

3 garlic cloves, minced
½ tsp salt
¼ tsp chilli powder

DIRECTIONS

Preheat your Air Fryer to 190°C. Toss the prawns with 2 tbsp of olive oil, lime juice, 1/3 of garlic, salt, and red chilli powder in a bowl. Mix the remaining olive oil and garlic in a small ramekin. Pour the prawns into the center of a piece of aluminum foil, then fold the sides up and crimp the edges so that it forms an aluminum foil bowl that is open on top. Put the resulting packet into the frying basket.

Dilly Jacket Potatoes

Serves: 4 | Total Time: 50 minutes

INGREDIENTS

2 russet potatoes
3 tbsp olive oil
Salt and pepper to taste
2 tbsp rosemary, chopped

10 Kalamata olives, diced
30g crumbled feta
2 tbsp chopped dill

DIRECTIONS

Preheat your Air Fryer to 190°C. Poke 2-3 holes in the potatoes with a fork. Drizzle them with some olive oil and sprinkle with salt. Put the potatoes into the frying basket and Bake for 30 minutes.

Remove the potatoes from the fryer and slice them in half when they are ready. Scoop out the flesh of the potatoes with a spoon, leaving a 1-cm layer of potato inside the skins, and set the skins aside.

Combine the scooped potato middles with olive oil, salt, black pepper, and rosemary in a medium bowl. Mix until well combined. Spoon the potato filling into the skins, spreading it evenly over them. Top with olives, dill, and feta. Put the loaded potato skins back into the air fryer and Bake for 15 minutes. Enjoy!

Spanish Fried Baby Squid

Serves: 2 | Total Time: 30 minutes

INGREDIENTS

120g baby squid
60g semolina flour
½ tsp Spanish paprika

2 eggs
Salt and pepper to taste
2 tbsp lemon juice

DIRECTIONS

Preheat your Air Fryer to 180°C. Beat the eggs in a bowl. Stir in lemon juice and set aside. Mix flour, paprika, salt, and pepper in another bowl. Dip each piece of squid into the flour, then into the eggs, and then again. Transfer them to the greased frying basket and Air Fry for 18-20 minutes, shaking the basket occasionally until crispy and golden brown. Serve hot.

Italian Basil and Tomato Bruschettas

Serves: 4 | Total Time: 15 minutes

INGREDIENTS

3 red tomatoes, diced
½ ciabatta loaf
1 fresh mozzarella ball, sliced
1 tbsp olive oil

10 fresh basil, chopped
1 tsp balsamic vinegar
Pinch of salt

DIRECTIONS

Preheat your Air Fryer to 185°C. Mix tomatoes, olive oil, salt, vinegar, and basil in a bowl until well combined. Cut the loaf into 6 slices, about 3-cm thick. Spoon the tomato mixture over the bread and top with one mozzarella slice. Repeat for all bruschettas. Put the bruschettas in the foil-lined frying basket and Bake for 5 minutes until golden. Serve.

Mexican Empanadas

Serves: 4 | Total Time: 20 minutes

INGREDIENTS

60g cooked black beans
30g white onions, diced
1 tsp red chilli powder

½ tsp salt
½ tsp cumin
4 empanada dough shells

DIRECTIONS

Preheat your Air Fryer to 175°C. Stir-fry black beans and onions in a pan over medium heat for 5 minutes. Add chilli, salt, and cumin. Set aside covered.

Lay the empanada shells on a clean workspace. Spoon bean mixture onto shells without spilling. Fold the shells over to cover fully. Seal the edges with water and press with a fork.

Transfer the empanadas to the foil-lined frying basket and Bake for 15 minutes, flipping once halfway through cooking. Cook until golden. Serve.

Stuffed Dates

Serves: 6 | Total Time: 20 minutes

INGREDIENTS

12 bacon slices, halved
24 pitted dates

3 tbsp crumbled blue cheese
1 tbsp cream cheese

DIRECTIONS

Make a slit lengthways in each date. Mix the blue cheese and cream cheese in a small bowl. Add ½ tsp of cheese mixture to the center of each date. Wrap each date with a slice of bacon and seal with a toothpick.

Preheat your Air Fryer to 200°C. Place the dates on the bottom of the greased frying basket in a single layer. Bake for 6-8 minutes, flipping the dates once until the bacon is cooked and crispy. Allow to cool and serve warm.

Spicy Two-Cheese Rolls

Serves: 4 | Total Time: 25 minutes

INGREDIENTS

30g grated cheddar cheese
30g blue cheese, crumbled
8 flaky pastry dough sheets

1 tbsp vegetable oil
1 tsp dry thyme

DIRECTIONS

Preheat your Air Fryer to 175°C. Mix the cheddar cheese, blue cheese, and thyme in a bowl. Divide the cheese mixture between pastry sheets and seal the seams with water.

Brush the pastry rolls with vegetable oil. Arrange them on the greased frying basket and Bake for 15 minutes or until the pastry crust is golden brown and the cheese is melted. Serve hot.

Garlicky Pita Crackers

Serves: 2 | Total Time: 15 minutes

INGREDIENTS

2 pitas, cut into wedges
1 tbsp olive oil
½ tsp salt

¼ tsp garlic powder
¼ tsp paprika

DIRECTIONS

Preheat your Air Fryer to 180°C. Coat the pita wedges with olive oil, paprika, salt, and garlic powder in a bowl. Put them into the frying basket and Air Fry for 6-8 minutes. Serve warm.

King Prawns Wrapped in Bacon

Serves: 4 | Total Time: 15 minutes

INGREDIENTS

2 king prawns, peeled
2 bacon strips, sliced
2 tbsp lemon juice

½ tsp chipotle powder
½ tsp garlic salt

DIRECTIONS

Preheat your Air Fryer to 180°C. Wrap the bacon around the prawns, and place the prawns in the foil-lined frying basket, seam side down. Drizzle with lemon juice, chipotle powder, and garlic salt. Air Fry for 10 minutes, turning the prawns once until cooked and the bacon crispy. Serve hot.

Hot Dog Rolls

Serves: 4 | Total Time: 25 minutes

INGREDIENTS

8 small mini hot dogs
8 pastry dough sheets

1 tbsp vegetable oil
1 tbsp poppy seeds

DIRECTIONS

Preheat your Air Fryer to 180°C. Roll the mini hot dogs into a pastry dough sheet, wrapping them snugly. Brush the rolls with vegetable oil on all sides. Arrange them on the frying basket and sprinkle poppy seeds on top. Bake for 15 minutes until the pastry crust is golden brown. Serve.

Chilli Chicken Wings

Serves: 6 | Total Time: 60 minutes

INGREDIENTS

1 kg chicken wings, split at the joint
1 tbsp butter, softened
60ml buffalo wing sauce

Salt and black pepper to taste
1 tsp red chilli powder
1 tsp garlic-ginger puree

DIRECTIONS

Preheat your Air Fryer to 200°C. Rub the chicken wings with salt, pepper, red chilli powder, and garlic-ginger puree. Place the chicken wings in the greased frying basket and Air Fry for 12 minutes, tossing once. Whisk butter and buffalo sauce in a large bowl. Air Fry for 10 more minutes, shaking once. Once done, transfer it into the bowl with the sauce. Serve immediately.

Thyme Sweet Potato Chips

Serves: 2 | Total Time: 20 minutes

INGREDIENTS

1 tbsp olive oil
1 sweet potato, sliced

¼ tsp dried thyme
Salt to taste

DIRECTIONS

Preheat your Air Fryer to 195°C. Spread the sweet potato slices in the greased basket and brush with olive oil. Air Fry for 6 minutes. Remove the basket, shake, and sprinkle with thyme and salt. Cook for 6 more minutes or until lightly browned. Serve warm and enjoy!

Parsley Breaded Artichoke Hearts

Serves: 6 | Total Time: 25 minutes

INGREDIENTS

12 tinned artichoke hearts
2 eggs
60g plain flour

40g panko bread crumbs
½ tsp dried parsley

DIRECTIONS

Preheat your Air Fryer to 190°C. Set out three small bowls. In the first, add flour. In the second, beat the eggs. In the third, mix the crumbs and parsley.

Dip the artichoke in the flour, dredge in the egg, then in the bread crumb. Place the breaded artichokes in the greased frying basket and Air Fry for 8 minutes, flipping them once until just browned and crisp. Allow to cool slightly and serve.

Cheesy Strips with Pimientos

Serves: 4 | Total Time: 35 minutes

INGREDIENTS

30g cream cheese

250g shredded sharp cheddar cheese

1 (120g) jar chopped pimientos, including juice

30g mayonnaise

Salt and pepper to taste

8 sandwich bread slices

2 tbsp olive oil

DIRECTIONS

In a bowl, mix the cream cheese, cheddar cheese, pimientos, mayonnaise, salt, and pepper. Let chill covered in the fridge for 30 minutes.

Preheat your Air Fryer to 180°C. Spread pimiento mixture over 4 bread slices, then top with the remaining slices and press down just enough to not smoosh cheese out of the sandwich edges.

Drizzle the top and bottom of each sandwich lightly with olive oil. Place sandwiches in the frying basket and Grill for 6 minutes, flipping once. Slice each sandwich into 16 sections and serve warm.

Basil Aubergine Fries

Serves: 4 | Total Time: 20 minutes

INGREDIENTS

1 aubergine, sliced

2 ½ tbsp shoyu

2 tsp garlic powder

2 tsp onion powder

4 tsp olive oil

2 tbsp fresh basil, chopped

DIRECTIONS

Preheat your Air Fryer to 195°C. Place the aubergine slices in a bowl and sprinkle the shoyu, garlic, onion, and oil. Coat the aubergine evenly. Place the aubergine in a single layer in the greased frying basket and Air Fry for 5 minutes. Remove and put the aubergine in the bowl again

Toss the aubergine slices to coat evenly with the remaining liquid and put back in the fryer. Roast for another 3 minutes. Remove the basket and flip the pieces over to ensure even cooking. Roast for another 5 minutes until the aubergine is golden. Top with basil and serve.

Honey-Mustard Pigs in Blankets

Serves: 4 | Total Time: 30 minutes

INGREDIENTS

250g crescent rolls

8 mini smoked hot dogs

30ml honey mustard

30ml mayonnaise

DIRECTIONS

Preheat your Air Fryer to 190°C. Roll out the crescent roll dough and separate into 8 triangles. Cut each triangle in half. Place 1 hot dog at the base of the triangle and roll it up in the dough; gently press the tip in. Repeat for the rest of the rolls. Place the rolls in the greased frying basket. Bake for 8-10 minutes. Mix the honey mustard and mayonnaise in a small bowl. Serve the hot dogs with the dip.

Morrocan Roasted Chickpeas

Serves: 3 | Total Time: 30 minutes

INGREDIENTS

2 tsp olive oil
450g tinned chickpeas
Salt to taste
1 tsp za'atar seasoning

1 tsp sumac
¼ tsp garlic powder
1 tbsp coriander, chopped

DIRECTIONS

Preheat your Air Fryer to 200°C. Combine salt, za´atar, sumac, and garlic powder in a bowl. Put half of the chickpeas in the greased frying basket. Bake for 12 minutes, shaking every 5, minutes until crunchy and golden brown. Transfer the chickpeas to a bowl. Lightly coat them with olive oil, then toss them with half of the spice mix while still hot. Serve topped with coriander.

Garlic Cocktail Beef Bites

Serves: 4 | Total Time: 30 minutes

INGREDIENTS

450g sirloin tip, cubed
200ml cheese pasta sauce
180g soft bread crumbs

2 tbsp olive oil
½ tsp garlic powder
½ tsp dried thyme

DIRECTIONS

Preheat your Air Fryer to 180°C. Toss the beef and the pasta sauce in a medium bowl. Set aside. In a shallow bowl, mix bread crumbs, oil, garlic, and thyme until well combined.

Drop the cubes into the crumb mixture to coat. Place them in the greased frying basket and Bake for 6-8 minutes, shaking once, until the beef is crisp and browned. Serve warm with toothpicks.

Courgette Boats with Havarti Cheese and Pancetta

Serves: 4 | Total Time: 35 minutes

INGREDIENTS

150g shredded Havarti cheese
3 pancetta slices
2 large courgettes

Salt and pepper to taste
¼ tsp sweet paprika
8 tsp Greek yogurt

DIRECTIONS

Preheat your Air Fryer to 180°C. Place the pancetta in the frying basket and Air Fry it for 10 minutes, flipping once until crisp. Chop the pancetta and set aside.

Cut the courgette in half lengthwise and then crosswise to have 8 pieces. Scoop out the pulp. Sprinkle with salt, paprika, and black pepper.

Place the courgette skins in the greased frying basket. Air Fry until crisp-tender, 8-10 minutes. Remove the basket, add Havarti cheese to each boat, and top with pancetta. Return stuffed boats to the air fryer and fry for 2 minutes or until the cheese has melted. Serve.

Sweet Potato Fries with Peach Chutney

Serves: 4 | Total Time: 20 minutes

INGREDIENTS

60ml sour cream
60g peach chutney
3 tsp curry powder

2 sweet potatoes, julienned
1 tbsp olive oil
Salt and pepper to taste

DIRECTIONS

Preheat your Air Fryer to 190°C. Mix together sour cream, peach chutney, and 1 ½ tsp curry powder in a small bowl. Set aside. In a medium bowl, add sweet potatoes, olive oil, the rest of the curry powder, salt, and pepper. Toss to coat. Place the potatoes in the frying basket.

Bake for about 6 minutes, then shake the basket once. Cook for an additional 4 -6 minutes or until the potatoes are golden and crispy. Serve the fries hot in a basket, along with the chutney sauce for dipping.

Paprika Onion Blossom

Serves: 4 | Total Time: 35 minutes + cooling time

INGREDIENTS

1 large onion
180g plain flour
1 tsp hot paprika

Salt and pepper to taste
2 eggs
120ml milk

DIRECTIONS

Remove the tip of the onion, but leave the root base intact. Peel the onion to the root and remove the skin. Place the onion cut side down on a cutting board. Start 1 cm down from the root and cut down to the bottom. Repeat until the onion is divided into quarters. Starting 1 cm down from the root, repeat the cuts in between the first cuts. Repeat this process between the cuts until you have 16 cuts in the onion. Flip the onion onto the root and carefully spread the inner layers. Set aside.

In a bowl, add flour, paprika, salt, and pepper, then stir. In another large bowl, whisk eggs and milk. Place the onion in the flour bowl and cover with flour mixture.

Transfer the onion to the egg mixture and coat thoroughly with a spoon or basting brush. Return the onion to the flour bowl and cover completely. Take a sheet of foil and wrap the onion with the foil. Freeze for 45 minutes.

Preheat your Air Fryer to 200°C. Remove the onion from the foil and place in the greased frying basket. Air Fry for 10 minutes. Lightly spray the onion with cooking oil, then cook for another 10-15 minutes.

Sticky Chicken Wings

Serves: 4 | Total Time: 30 minutes

INGREDIENTS

8 chicken wings
1 tbsp olive oil
3 tbsp brown sugar

2 tbsp maple syrup
60ml apple cider vinegar
Salt to taste

DIRECTIONS

Preheat your Air Fryer to 195°C. Toss the wings with olive oil in a bowl. Bake in the air fryer for 20 minutes, shaking the basket twice. While the chicken is cooking, whisk together sugar, maple syrup, vinegar, and salt in a small bowl. Transfer the wings to a baking pan, then pour the sauce over the wings. Toss well to coat. Cook in the air fryer until the wings are glazed or for another 5 minutes. Serve hot.

Mediterranean Curly Kale Chips

Serves: 4 | Total Time: 15 minutes

INGREDIENTS

150g Greek yogurt
3 tbsp lemon juice
1 tbsp minced walnuts

1 curly kale bunch
2 tbsp olive oil
Salt and pepper to taste

DIRECTIONS

Preheat your Air Fryer to 190°C. Mix together yogurt, lemon juice, and walnuts until well blended. Set aside. Cut off the stems and ribs from the kale and then the leaves into 7 cm pieces. In a bowl, toss the kale with olive oil, salt, and pepper. Arrange the kale in the fryer and Air Fry for 2-3 minutes. Shake the basket, then cook for another 2-3 minutes or until the kale is crisp. Serve the chips with Greek sauce.

Cinnamon Sweet Potato Fries

Serves: 5 | Total Time: 30 minutes

INGREDIENTS

3 sweet potatoes
2 tsp butter, melted

1 tsp cinnamon
Salt and pepper to taste

DIRECTIONS

Preheat your Air Fryer to 200°C. Peel the potatoes and slice them thinly crosswise. Transfer the slices to a large bowl. Toss with butter, cinnamon, salt, and pepper until fully coated. Place half of the slices into the air fryer. Stacking is ok. Air Fry for 10 minutes. Shake the basket, and cook for another 10-12 minutes until crispy. Serve hot.

Honey Bacon Tater Tots

Serves: 4 | Total Time: 25 minutes

INGREDIENTS

24 frozen tater tots
6 bacon slices

1 tbsp honey
120g grated cheddar

DIRECTIONS

Preheat your Air Fryer to 200°C. Air Fry the tater tots for 10 minutes, shaking the basket once halfway through cooking. Cut the bacon into pieces. When the tater tots are done, remove them from the fryer to a baking pan. Top them with bacon and drizzle with honey. Air Fry for 5 minutes to crisp up the bacon. Top the tater tots with cheese and cook for 2 minutes to melt the cheese. Serve.

Tomatillo Salsa Verde

Serves: 4 | Total Time: 35 minutes + cooling time

INGREDIENTS

2 tbsp olive oil
2 serrano peppers
1 small onion, quartered
450g tomatillos, husks removed

3 tsp chopped coriander
1 tsp lime juice
½ tsp salt

DIRECTIONS

Preheat your Air Fryer to 190°C. Place the serrano peppers, onion, and tomatillos onto a baking sheet pan and lightly drizzle them with olive oil. Insert the sheet in the air fryer and Roast for 13-15 minutes, turning everything halfway through until blistered.

Remove the sheet from the fryer and add the tomatillos, onion, coriander, lime juice, and salt to your blender. Wrap the peppers in foil and let them cool for a few minutes. Peel and discard the skin of the garlic and unwrap the peppers. Cut the serrano peppers in half and remove the seeds.

Add the garlic and peppers to the blender. Pulse until coarsely chopped. Slowly add 2-3 tbsp of water and pulse again to combine until smooth and pureed. Keep in the refrigerator until ready to use.

Garlic Kale Chips

Serves: 6 | Total Time: 20 minutes

INGREDIENTS

1 tbsp chilli powder
1 tsp garlic powder
400g kale, torn

3 tsp olive oil
Sea salt to taste

DIRECTIONS

Preheat your Air Fryer to 195°C. Mix the garlic and chilli powders. Coat the kale with olive oil. Put it in the frying basket and Air Fry until crispy, about 5-6 minutes, shaking the basket at around 3 minutes. Toss some sea salt on the kale chips once they are finished. Serve.

Tomato Roasted Potatoes

Serves: 4 | Total Time: 25 minutes

INGREDIENTS

16 cherry tomatoes, halved
6 red potatoes, cubed
3 garlic cloves, minced

Salt and pepper to taste
1 tsp chopped chives
1 tbsp extra-virgin olive oil

DIRECTIONS

Preheat your Air Fryer to 200°C. Combine cherry potatoes, garlic, salt, pepper, chives, and olive oil in a resealable plastic bag. Seal and shake the bag. Put the potatoes in the greased frying basket and Roast for 10 minutes. Shake the basket, place the cherry tomatoes in, and cook for 10 more minutes. Allow to cool slightly and serve.

Cheese and Bacon Potato Canapés

Serves: 4 | Total Time: 35 minutes

INGREDIENTS

4 bacon slices
4 russet potatoes, sliced
1 tbsp olive oil

1 tsp mustard powder
Salt and pepper to taste
120g grated cheddar cheese

DIRECTIONS

Cook bacon in a skillet for 5 minutes over medium heat. Drain on a paper towel and crumble. Set aside. Add the potatoes to a large bowl and coat them with olive oil, mustard powder, salt, and pepper.

Preheat your Air Fryer to 200°C. Place the potatoes in the greased frying basket. Air Fry for 10 minutes. Shake the basket and cook for another 5-8 minutes or until the potatoes are cooked through and the edges are crisp. Transfer the potato bites to a serving dish. Serve warm, topped with cheese and bacon.

Easy Italian Pickle Crisps

Serves: 4 | Total Time: 20 minutes

INGREDIENTS

450g dill pickles, sliced
2 eggs
40g flour

40g breadcrumbs
1 tsp Italian seasoning

DIRECTIONS

Preheat your Air Fryer to 200°C. Set out three small bowls. In the first bowl, add flour. In the second bowl, beat eggs. In the third bowl, mix bread crumbs with Italian seasoning.

Dip the pickle slices in the flour. Shake, then dredge in egg. Roll in bread crumbs and shake excess. Place the pickles in the greased frying basket and Air Fry for 6 minutes. Flip them halfway through cooking and fry for another 3 minutes until crispy. Serve.

Chicken Mini Meatballs

Serves: 4 | Total Time: 30 minutes

INGREDIENTS

2 tsp olive oil
30g onion, minced
¼ red pepper, minced

3 tsp grated Parmesan cheese
1 egg white
200g minced chicken

DIRECTIONS

Preheat your Air Fryer to 185°C. Combine the olive oil, onion, and red pepper in a baking pan, then transfer to the air fryer. Bake for 3-5 minutes until tender. Add the cooked vegetables, Parmesan cheese, egg white, and minced chicken to a bowl and stir.

Form the mixture into small meatballs and put them in the frying basket. Air Fry for 10-15 minutes, shaking the basket once until the meatballs are crispy and brown on all sides. Serve warm.

Tasty Fried Olives

Serves: 4 | Total Time: 25 minutes

INGREDIENTS

150g jarred pitted green olives
60g plain flour
Salt and pepper to taste

1 tsp Greek seasoning
60g bread crumbs
1 egg

DIRECTIONS

Preheat your Air Fryer to 200°C. Set out three small bowls. In the first, mix flour, Greek seasoning, salt, and pepper. In the bowl, beat the egg. In the third bowl, add bread crumbs.

Dip the olives in the flour, then the egg, then in the crumbs. When all the olives are breaded, place them in the greased frying basket and Air Fry for 6 minutes. Turn them and cook for another 2 minutes or until brown and crispy. Serve chilled.

Chilli Okra Fries

Serves: 4 | Total Time: 25 minutes

INGREDIENTS

200g trimmed okra, cut lengthways
¼ tsp chilli powder
3 tbsp buttermilk

2 tbsp chickpea flour
2 tbsp cornmeal
Salt and pepper to taste

DIRECTIONS

Preheat your Air Fryer to 190°C. Set out 2 bowls. In one, add buttermilk. In the second, mix flour, cornmeal, chilli powder, salt, and pepper. Dip the okra in buttermilk, then dredge in flour and cornmeal. Transfer to the frying basket and spray the okra with oil. Air Fry for 10 minutes, shaking once halfway through cooking until crispy. Let cool it for a few minutes. Serve warm.

Jalapeno Stuffed Mushrooms

Serves: 4 | Total Time: 30 minutes

INGREDIENTS

16 button mushrooms
40ml salsa
1 onion, finely chopped

1 jalapeño pepper, minced
3 tbsp shredded mozzarella
2 tsp olive oil

DIRECTIONS

Preheat your Air Fryer to 175°C. Cut the stem off the mushrooms, then slice them finely. Set the caps aside. Combine the salsa, onion, jalapeño, and mozzarella cheese in a bowl, then add the stems.

Fill the mushroom caps with the mixture, making sure to overfill so the mix is coming out of the top. Drizzle with olive oil. Place the caps in the air fryer and Bake for 8-12 minutes. The filling should be hot and the mushrooms soft. Serve warm.

Sesame Chicken Wings

Serves: 4 | Total Time: 30 minutes

INGREDIENTS

8 chicken wings
Salt and pepper to taste
3 tbsp honey

2 cloves garlic, minced
100ml barbecue sauce
1 tbsp sesame seeds

DIRECTIONS

Preheat your Air Fryer to 195°C. Season the wings with salt and pepper and place them in the frying basket. Air Fry for 20 minutes. Shake the basket a couple of times during cooking. In a bowl, mix the honey, 1 tbsp of water, and garlic. Take the wings out of the fryer and place them in a baking pan.

Add the sauce and toss, coating completely. Put the pan in the air fryer and Air Fry for 4-5 minutes until golden and cooked through, with no pink showing. Top with sesame seeds, then serve with BBQ sauce.

Bacon and Blue Cheese Tartlets

Serves: 6 | Total Time: 30 minutes

INGREDIENTS

6 bacon slices
16 phyllo tartlet shells

60g diced blue cheese
3 tbsp apple jelly

DIRECTIONS

Preheat your Air Fryer to 200°C. Put the bacon in a single layer in the frying basket and Air Fry for 14 minutes, turning once halfway through. Remove and drain on paper towels, then crumble when cool. Wipe the fryer clean. Fill the tartlet shells with bacon and the blue cheese cubes, and add a dab of apple jelly on top of the filling. Lower the temperature to 175°C, then put the shells in the frying basket. Air Fry until the cheese melts and the shells brown, about 5-6 minutes. Remove and serve.

Smoked Piri Piri Chicken Drumettes

Serves: 4 | Total Time: 45 minutes

INGREDIENTS

120g crushed cracker crumbs
1 tbsp smoked paprika
1 tbsp Piri Piri seasoning
1 tsp salt

1 tsp garlic powder
1 kg chicken drumettes
2 tbsp olive oil

DIRECTIONS

Preheat your Air Fryer to 190°C. Combine the cracker crumbs, smoked paprika, Piri Piri seasoning, salt, and garlic powder in a bowl and mix well. Pour into a screw-top glass jar and set aside.

Put the drumettes in a large bowl, drizzle with the olive oil, and toss to coat. Sprinkle 1/3 cup of the breading mix over the meat and press the mix into the drumettes.

Put half the drumettes in the frying basket and Air Fry for 20-25 minutes, shaking the basket once until golden and crisp. Serve hot.

Simple Deviled Eggs

Serves 4 | Total Time: 20 minutes

INGREDIENTS

4 eggs
2 tbsp mayonnaise
10 chopped Nicoise olives

2 tbsp goat cheese crumbles
Salt and pepper to taste
2 tbsp chopped parsley

DIRECTIONS

Preheat your Air Fryer to 130°C. Place the eggs in silicone muffin cups to avoid bumping around and cracking during cooking. Add silicone cups to the frying basket and Air Fry for 15 minutes. Remove and run the eggs under cold water. When cool, remove the shells and halve them lengthwise.

Spoon yolks into a separate medium bowl and arrange white halves on a large plate. Mash the yolks with a fork. Stir in the remaining ingredients. Spoon mixture into white halves and top with mint. Serve.

Coriander-Avocado Balls

Serves: 6 | Total Time: 25 minutes + freezing time

INGREDIENTS

2 avocados, peeled
1 tbsp minced coriander
½ tsp salt

1 egg, beaten
1 tbsp milk
60g almond flour

DIRECTIONS

Mash the avocados in a bowl with coriander and salt. Line a baking sheet with parchment paper and form the mix into 12 balls. Use an ice cream scoop or ⅛-cup measure. Put them on the baking sheet and freeze for 2 hours. Beat the egg with milk in a shallow bowl.

Preheat your Air Fryer to 200°C. Dip the frozen guac balls in the egg mix, then roll them in the almond flour, coating evenly. Put half the bombs in the freezer while you cook the first group.

The other 6 go in the frying basket. Mist with olive oil and Air Fry for 4-5 minutes or until golden. Repeat with the second batch and serve.

Brie and Bacon Spread

Serves: 6 | Total Time: 30 minutes

INGREDIENTS

120g cream cheese, softened
3 tbsp mayonnaise
120g diced Brie cheese

120g cooked bacon, crumbled
40g dried currants

DIRECTIONS

Preheat your Air Fryer to 180°C. Beat the cream cheese with the mayo until well blended. Stir in the Brie, bacon, and currants, and pour the dip mix into a 15-cm round pan.Put the pan in the fryer and Air Fry for 10-12 minutes, stirring once until the dip melts and bubbles. Serve warm.

Aubergine Sticks with Parmesan

Serves 4 | Total Time: 35 minutes

INGREDIENTS

2 eggs, whisked
60g bread crumbs
60g grated Parmesan cheese

½ tsp salt
1 aubergine, cut into sticks
60ml tomato sauce, warm

DIRECTIONS

Preheat your Air Fryer to 200°C.

In a bowl, combine bread crumbs, Parmesan cheese, and salt. Dip aubergine fries in whisked eggs and dredge them in the crumb mixture.

Place the fries in the greased frying basket and Air Fry for 12 minutes, shaking once. Transfer to a large serving plate and serve with warmed tomato sauce.

Beetroot Fries

Serves: 4 | Total Time: 40 minutes

INGREDIENTS

2 peeled beetroots
Salt to taste
2 eggs

120g panko bread crumbs
½ tsp paprika

DIRECTIONS

Preheat your Air Fryer to 185°C.

Slice the beetroots into 7 cm long sticks that are 1 cm thick. Beat the eggs in a shallow bowl and combine the panko and paprika on a plate.

Dip the fries in the egg, then the panko mixture, coating well. Put the beetroots in the frying basket and spray with cooking oil. Air Fry for 18-23 minutes or until crispy and golden. Serve.

Lime Corn on the Cob

Serves: 4 | Total Time: 30 minutes

INGREDIENTS

Salt and pepper to taste
4 corn ears, halved
1 tbsp butter, melted

30ml lime juice
1 tsp lime zest
1 lime, quartered

DIRECTIONS

Preheat your Air Fryer to 200°C.

Combine salt, pepper, lime juice, and zest in a small bowl. Toss corn and butter in a large bowl, then add the seasonings from the small bowl. Toss until coated.

Arrange the corn in a single layer in the frying basket. Air Fry for 10 minutes, then turn the corn. Air Fry for another 8 minutes. Squeeze lime over the corn and serve.

Rosemary Cheesy Bake

Serves 4 | Total Time: 20 minutes

INGREDIENTS

2 peeled garlic cloves roasted
180g goat cheese
60g grated Parmesan cheese
1 egg, beaten

1 tbsp olive oil
Salt and pepper to taste
1 tsp chopped rosemary

DIRECTIONS

Preheat your Air Fryer to 180°C. Carefully squeeze the garlic into a bowl and mash it with a fork until a paste is formed. Stir in goat cheese, Parmesan cheese, egg, olive oil, salt, black pepper, and rosemary. Spoon the mixture into a baking dish and place the dish in the frying basket. Air Fry for 7 minutes.

Breaded Mozzarella Sticks

Serves 6 | Total Time: 25 minutes

INGREDIENTS

2 tbsp flour
1 egg
1 tbsp milk
½ breadcrumbs

¼ tsp salt
10 mozzarella sticks
2 tsp olive oil

DIRECTIONS

Place the flour in a bowl. In another bowl, beat the egg and milk. In a third bowl, combine the crumbs with salt. Cut the mozzarella sticks into thirds.

Roll each piece in flour, dredge in egg mixture, and roll in breadcrumb mixture. Shake off the excess between each step. Place them in the freezer for 10 minutes.

Preheat your Air Fryer to 200°C. Place mozzarella sticks in the frying basket and Air Fry for 5 minutes, shake twice, and brush with olive oil. Serve the mozzarella sticks immediately.

Quick Parmesan Asparagus

Serves: 4 | Total Time: 15 minutes

INGREDIENTS

3 tsp grated Parmesan cheese
500g asparagus, trimmed
2 tsp olive oil

Salt to taste
1 clove garlic, minced
½ lemon

DIRECTIONS

Preheat your Air Fryer to 190°C. Toss the asparagus and olive oil in a bowl, place them in the frying basket, and Air Fry for 8-10 minutes, tossing once. Transfer them to a large serving dish.

Sprinkle with salt, garlic, and Parmesan cheese and toss until coated. Serve immediately with a squeeze of lemon. Enjoy!

POULTRY RECIPES

Chessy Chicken Strips

Serves: 4 | Total Time: 40 minutes

INGREDIENTS

1 chicken breast, sliced into strips
1 tbsp grated Parmesan cheese
120g breadcrumbs

1 tbsp chicken seasoning
2 eggs, beaten
Salt and pepper to taste

DIRECTIONS

Preheat your Air Fryer to 175°C. Mix the breadcrumbs, Parmesan cheese, chicken seasoning, salt, and pepper in a mixing bowl. Coat the chicken with the crumb mixture, then dip in the beaten eggs. Finally, coat again with the dry ingredients. Arrange the coated chicken pieces on the greased frying basket and Air Fry for 15 minutes. Turn over halfway through cooking and cook for another 15 minutes. Serve.

Lemon Drumettes

Serves: 2 | Total Time: 30 minutes + marinating time

INGREDIENTS

450g chicken drumettes
150ml buttermilk
100g bread crumbs

½ tsp smoked paprika
Salt and pepper to taste
3 tsp lemon juice

DIRECTIONS

Mix drumettes and buttermilk in a bowl and let sit covered in the fridge overnight. Preheat your Air Fryer to 175°C. In a bowl, combine the remaining ingredients. Shake excess buttermilk off drumettes and dip them in the breadcrumb mixture. Place breaded drumettes in the greased frying basket and Air Fry for 12 minutes. Increase the air fryer temperature to 200°C, toss the chicken, and cook for 8 minutes. Let rest for 5 minutes before serving.

Cornflake Chicken Nuggets

Serves: 4 | Total Time: 25 minutes

INGREDIENTS

1 egg white
Salt and pepper to taste
½ tsp paprika

450g chicken breast fingers
60g ground cornflakes
2 bread slices, crumbled

DIRECTIONS

Preheat your Air Fryer to 200°C. Whisk the egg white with salt, pepper, and paprika. Add the chicken and toss coat. Combine the cornflakes and breadcrumbs on a plate, then put the chicken fingers in the mix to coat. Put the nuggets in the frying basket and Air Fry for 10-13 minutes, turning halfway through until golden, crisp, and cooked through. Serve hot.

Chicken Roulades

Serves: 4 | Total Time: 35 minutes

INGREDIENTS

½ green pepper, cut into strips
1 carrot, cut into strips
4 chicken breast halves

½ lime, juiced
2 tbsp adobo seasoning

DIRECTIONS

Preheat your Air Fryer to 200°C. Place the chicken breasts between two plastic wraps and gently pound with a rolling pin to 0.5-cm thickness. Drizzle with lime juice and season with adobo seasoning.

Divide the carrot and green pepper equally between the 4 breasts. Roll up each chicken breast and secure it with toothpicks. Place the roulades in the frying basket and lightly spray with cooking oil. Bake for 12 minutes, turning once. Serve warm.

Butter Chicken Thighs

Serves: 4 | Total Time: 30 minutes

INGREDIENTS

4 bone-in chicken thighs, skinless
2 tbsp butter, melted
1 tsp garlic powder

1 tsp lemon zest
Salt and pepper to taste
1 lemon, sliced

DIRECTIONS

Preheat your Air Fryer to 190°C. Rub the chicken thighs with butter, lemon zest, garlic powder, and salt. Divide the chicken thighs between 4 pieces of foil and sprinkle with black pepper. Top with slices of lemon. Bake in the air fryer for 20-22 minutes until golden. Serve.

Chicken Parmigiana

Serves: 2 | Total Time: 35 minutes

INGREDIENTS

2 chicken breasts
100g breadcrumbs
2 eggs, beaten

Salt and pepper to taste
120ml passata
1 tbsp Parmesan cheese

DIRECTIONS

Preheat your Air Fryer to 175°C. Mix the breadcrumbs, salt, and pepper in a mixing bowl. Coat the chicken breasts with the crumb mixture, then dip in the beaten eggs.

Finally, coat again with the dry ingredients. Arrange the coated chicken breasts on the greased frying basket and Air Fry for 20 minutes. At the 10-minute mark, turn the breasts over and cook for the remaining 10 minutes.

Pour half of the passata into a baking pan. When the chicken is ready, remove it from the passata-covered pan. Pour the remaining passata over the fried chicken and sprinkle with Parmesan cheese. Bake for 5 minutes until the chicken is crisped and the cheese is melted and lightly toasted. Serve.

Chorizo and Chicken Empanadas

Serves: 4 | Total Time: 25 minutes

INGREDIENTS

120g chorizo sausage, casings removed and crumbled

1 tbsp olive oil

120g chicken breasts, diced

30g black olives, sliced

30g raisins

4 empanada shells

DIRECTIONS

Preheat your Air Fryer to 175°C. Warm the oil in a skillet over medium heat. Sauté the chicken and chorizo, breaking up the chorizo, 3-4 minutes. Add the raisins and olives and stir.

Kill the heat and let the mixture cool slightly. Divide the chorizo mixture between the empanada shells and fold them to cover the filling. Seal edges with water and press down with a fork to secure. Place the empanadas in the frying basket. Bake for 15 minutes, flipping once until golden. Serve warm.

Chicken Pie with Asparagus

Serves: 4 | Total Time: 30 minutes

INGREDIENTS

1 grilled chicken breast, diced

60g shredded Gruyère cheese

1 premade pie crust

2 eggs, beaten

Salt and pepper to taste

200g asparagus, sliced

DIRECTIONS

Preheat your Air Fryer to 180°C. Carefully press the crust into a baking dish, trimming the edges. Prick the dough with a fork a few times. Add the eggs, asparagus, salt, pepper, chicken, and half of Gruyère cheese to a mixing bowl and stir until thoroughly blended.

Pour the mixture into the pie crust. Bake in the air fryer for 15 minutes. Sprinkle the remaining Gruyère cheese on top of the quiche filling. Bake for 5 more minutes until the quiche is golden brown. Remove and allow to cool for a few minutes before cutting. Serve sliced, and enjoy!

Smoky Chicken Legs

Serves 4 | Total Time: 50 minutes

INGREDIENTS

1 tsp dried mustard

1 tsp smoked paprika

1 tsp garlic powder

1 tsp dried thyme

Salt and pepper to taste

700g chicken legs

3 tbsp olive oil

DIRECTIONS

Preheat your Air Fryer to 185°C. Combine all ingredients except olive oil in a bowl until coated. Place the chicken legs in the frying basket and brush with olive oil. Air Fry for 18 minutes, flipping once. Let chill on a serving plate for 5 minutes before serving.

Mango-Rubbed Chicken Legs

Serves: 3 | Total Time: 35 minutes

INGREDIENTS

120g Cajun seasoning
½ tsp mango powder

6 chicken legs, bone-in

DIRECTIONS

Preheat your Air Fryer to 180°C. Place half of the Cajun seasoning and 200ml water in a bowl and mix well to dissolve any lumps. Add the remaining Cajun seasoning and mango powder to a shallow bowl and stir to combine. Dip the chicken in the batter, then coat it in the mango seasoning. Lightly spritz the chicken with cooking spray. Place the chicken in the air fryer and Air Fry for 14-16 minutes, turning once until the chicken is cooked and the coating is brown. Serve and enjoy!

Chipotle Drumsticks

Serves: 4 | Total Time: 40 minutes

INGREDIENTS

150g tinned chipotle chillies packed in adobe sauce
2 tbsp grated Mexican cheese
6 chicken drumsticks
1 egg, beaten

60g bread crumbs
Salt and pepper to taste

DIRECTIONS

Preheat your Air Fryer to 175°C. Place the chillies in the sauce in your blender and pulse until a fine paste is formed. Transfer to a bowl and add the beaten egg. Combine thoroughly. Mix the breadcrumbs, Mexican cheese, salt, and pepper separately and set aside.

Coat the chicken drumsticks with the crumb mixture, dip them into the bowl with wet ingredients, then dip them again into the dry ingredients. Arrange the chicken drumsticks on the greased frying basket in a flat layer. Air Fry for 14-16 minutes, turning each chicken drumstick over once. Serve warm.

Tabasco Chicken Wings

Serves: 2 | Total Time: 40 minutes

INGREDIENTS

450g chicken wings
60g melted butter
3 tbsp Tabasco sauce

1 tsp garlic powder
1 tsp adobo seasoning
Salt and pepper to taste

DIRECTIONS

Preheat your Air Fryer to 175°C. Place the melted butter, Tabasco sauce, garlic, adobo seasoning, salt, and pepper in a bowl and stir to combine.

Dip the chicken wings into the mixture, coating thoroughly. Lay the coated chicken wings on the foil-lined frying basket in an even layer. Air Fry for 16-18 minutes. Shake the basket several times during cooking until the chicken wings are crispy brown.

Basil Chicken Pizzadillas

Serves: 4 | Total Time: 25 minutes

INGREDIENTS

300g cooked boneless, skinless chicken meat, shredded

8 basil leaves, julienned

½ tsp salt

3 tbsp olive oil

8 flour tortillas

150ml marinara sauce

240g grated cheddar cheese

DIRECTIONS

Preheat your Air Fryer to 180°C. Sprinkle the chicken with salt. Drizzle one side of a tortilla lightly with olive oil. Spread ¼-th of marinara sauce, then top with ¼-th of chicken, ¼-th of cheddar cheese, and finally, ¼-th of basil leaves

Top with a second tortilla and lightly drizzle the top with olive oil. Repeat with the remaining ingredients. Put the quesadillas in the fryer and Bake for 3 minutes. Cut them into 6 sections and serve.

Mustardy Chicken Fingers

Serves: 4 | Total Time: 30 minutes

INGREDIENTS

450g chicken breast fingers

1 tbsp chicken seasoning

½ tsp mustard powder

Salt and pepper to taste

2 eggs

120g bread crumbs

DIRECTIONS

Preheat your Air Fryer to 200°C. Add the chicken fingers to a large bowl along with chicken seasoning, mustard, salt, and pepper; mix well. Set up two small bowls. In one bowl, beat the eggs.

In the second bowl, add the bread crumbs. Dip the chicken in the egg, then dredge in breadcrumbs. Place the nuggets in the air fryer. Lightly spray with cooking oil, then Air Fry for 8 minutes, shaking the basket once until crispy and cooked through. Serve warm.

Greek Chicken Wings

Serves: 4 | Total Time: 30 minutes

INGREDIENTS

8 whole chicken wings

½ lemon, juiced

½ tsp Greek seasoning

Salt and pepper to taste

30ml buttermilk

60g plain flour

DIRECTIONS

Preheat your Air Fryer to 200°C. Put the wings in a resealable bag along with lemon juice, Greek seasoning, salt, and pepper. Seal the bag and shake to coat. Set up bowls large enough to fit the wings.

In one bowl, pour the buttermilk. In the other, add flour. Dip the wings into the buttermilk using tongs, then dredge in flour. Transfer the wings to the greased frying basket, spraying lightly with cooking oil. Air Fry for 25 minutes, shaking twice, until golden and cooked through. Serve.

Stuffed Chicken Meatballs with Cheese

Serves: 4 | Total Time: 20 minutes

INGREDIENTS

1 tbsp cream cheese
3 tsp grated cheddar cheese
Salt and pepper to taste
450g minced chicken

¼ tsp chilli powder
120g bread crumbs
2 tbsp olive oil

DIRECTIONS

In a bowl, combine the cream cheese and cheddar cheese. Shape the mixture into 8 balls. Also, mix the minced chicken, chilli, salt, and pepper in a bowl. Divide into 8 meatballs.

Form a hole in each chicken meatball and place a cheese ball into the hole. Mold the chicken up and around to enclose the cheese balls until completely covered. Repeat the process until you run out of ingredients.

Preheat your Air Fryer to 190°C. Mix the breadcrumbs and salt in a bowl. Roll stuffed meatballs in the mixture and brush them with some olive oil. Place the meatballs in the greased frying basket. Air Fry for 6-8 minutes. Slide out the basket, turn the balls, and brush them with the remaining olive oil. Continue cooking for another 6 minutes. Serve immediately and enjoy!

Mustard Chicken Breasts

Serves: 4 | Total Time: 20 minutes

INGREDIENTS

½ tsp granulated garlic
½ tsp chilli powder
¼ tsp sweet paprika

Salt and pepper to taste
450g chicken breasts, sliced
2 tbsp yellow mustard

DIRECTIONS

Preheat your Air Fryer to 190°C. Mix together salt, garlic, chilli powder, paprika, and black pepper in a small bowl. Coat the chicken with mustard in a bowl. Sprinkle the seasoning mix over the chicken. Place the chicken in the greased frying basket and Air Fry for 7-8, flipping once until cooked through.

Tasty Chicken Bites

Serves: 4 | Total Time: 20 minutes + chilling time

INGREDIENTS

2 tbsp horseradish mustard
1 tbsp mayonnaise
1 tbsp olive oil

2 chicken breasts, cubes
1 tbsp parsley

DIRECTIONS

Combine all ingredients, excluding parsley, in a bowl. Let marinate covered in the fridge for 30 minutes. Preheat your Air Fryer to 175°C. Place chicken cubes in the greased frying basket and Air Fry for 9 minutes, tossing once. Serve immediately, sprinkled with parsley.

Jalapeño Chicken

Serves: 4 | Total Time: 30 minutes

INGREDIENTS

450g chicken breasts, cubed
100g mixed pepper strips
1 jalapeño pepper, minced

2 tsp olive oil
100g tinned black beans
75g salsa

DIRECTIONS

Preheat your Air Fryer to 200°C. Combine the chicken, pepper strips, jalapeño pepper, and olive oil in a bowl. Transfer to a bowl to the frying basket and Air Fry for 10 minutes, stirring once during cooking. When done, stir in black beans and salsa. Air Fry for 7-10 minutes or until cooked through. Serve warm.

Chicken Wings with Chilli Flakes

Serves: 4 | Total Time: 30 minutes

INGREDIENTS

16 chicken wings
1 tsp garlic powder
Salt and black pepper to taste

60g flour
30ml sour cream
2 tsp red chilli flakes

DIRECTIONS

Preheat your Air Fryer to 200°C. Put the wings in a resealable bag with garlic powder, salt, and pepper. Seal the bag and shake until the chicken is completely coated. Prepare a clean, resealable bag and add the flour. Pour sour cream into a large bowl.

Dunk the wings into the sour cream, then transfer them to the bag of flour. Seal the bag and shake until coated. Transfer the wings to the frying basket. Lightly spray them with cooking oil and Air Fry for 20-25 minutes, shaking the basket until crispy and golden brown. Remove to a plate and allow to cool slightly. Sprinkle with red chilli flakes. Serve and enjoy!

Thyme Chicken Breasts

Serves: 4 | Total Time: 30 minutes

INGREDIENTS

2 tbsp olive oil
3 tbsp balsamic vinegar
3 garlic cloves, minced
1 tsp thyme, chopped

1 tomato, diced
Salt and pepper to taste
4 chicken breasts

DIRECTIONS

Preheat your Air Fryer to 185°C. Combine the olive oil, balsamic vinegar, garlic, thyme, and tomato in a medium bowl. Set aside.

Cut 4-5 slits into the chicken breasts ¾ of the way through. Season salt and pepper and place the chicken with the slits facing up in the greased frying basket. Bake for 7 minutes. Spoon the thyme mixture into the slits of the chicken. Cook for another 3 minutes. Allow chicken to sit and cool for a few minutes.

Tuscan Chicken Roll-Ups

Serves: 4 | Total Time: 30 minutes

INGREDIENTS

30g ricotta cheese
100g Tuscan kale, chopped
4 chicken breasts

1 tbsp chicken seasoning
Salt and pepper to taste
1 tsp paprika

DIRECTIONS

Preheat your Air Fryer to 185°C. Soften the ricotta cheese in a microwave-safe bowl for 15 seconds. Combine in a bowl along with Tuscan kale. Set aside. Cut 4-5 slits in the top of each chicken breast about ¾ of the way down. Season with chicken seasoning, salt, and pepper.

Place the chicken with the slits facing up in the greased frying basket. Lightly spray the chicken with oil. Bake for 6-8 minutes. Slide-out and stuff the cream cheese mixture into the chicken slits. Sprinkle ½ tsp of paprika and cook for another 3 minutes. Serve and enjoy!

Sweet Chicken Drumsticks

Serves: 4 | Total Time: 45 minutes

INGREDIENTS

450g chicken drumsticks
1 tbsp chicken seasoning
1 tsp dried chilli flakes

Salt and pepper to taste
30g honey
150ml barbecue sauce

DIRECTIONS

Preheat your Air Fryer to 195°C. Season drumsticks with chicken seasoning, chilli flakes, salt, and pepper. Place one batch of drumsticks in the greased frying basket and Air Fry for 18-20 minutes, flipping once until golden.

While the chicken is cooking, combine honey and barbecue sauce in a small bowl. Remove the drumsticks to a serving dish. Drizzle honey-barbecue sauce over and serve.

Dijon Chicken Thighs

Serves: 4 | Total Time: 35 minutes

INGREDIENTS

8 boneless, skinless chicken thighs
Salt and pepper to taste
2 garlic cloves, minced

½ tsp apple cider vinegar
60ml honey
30g Dijon mustard

DIRECTIONS

Preheat your Air Fryer to 200°C. Season the chicken with salt and black pepper. Place in the greased frying basket and Bake for 15 minutes, flipping once halfway through cooking.

While the chicken is cooking, add garlic, honey, vinegar, and Dijon mustard in a saucepan and stir-fry over medium heat for 4 minutes or until the sauce has thickened and warmed through. Transfer the thighs to a serving dish and drizzle with honey-mustard sauce. Serve and enjoy!

Popcorn Chicken Tenders with Veggies

Serves: 4 | Total Time: 30 minutes

INGREDIENTS

2 tbsp cooked popcorn, ground
Salt and pepper to taste
450g chicken tenders
60g bread crumbs

1 tbsp olive oil
2 carrots, sliced
12 baby potatoes

DIRECTIONS

Preheat your Air Fryer to 190°C. Season the chicken tenders with salt and pepper. In a shallow bowl, mix the crumbs, popcorn, and olive oil until combined. Coat the chicken with the mixture.

Press firmly so the crumbs adhere. Arrange the carrots and baby potatoes in the greased frying basket and top them with the chicken tenders. Bake for 9-10 minutes. Shake the basket and continue cooking for another 9-10 minutes until the vegetables are tender. Serve and enjoy!

Sweet Chilli Chicken

Serves: 4 | Total Time: 30 minutes

INGREDIENTS

2 chicken breasts, cut into 3-cm pieces
120ml cornflour
1 tsp chicken seasoning
Salt and pepper to taste

2 eggs
150ml sweet chilli sauce

DIRECTIONS

Preheat your Air Fryer to 180°C. Mix cornflour, chicken seasoning, salt, and pepper in a large bowl. In another bowl, beat the eggs. Dip the chicken in the cornflour mixture to coat. Next, dip the chicken into the egg, then return to the cornflour. Transfer the chicken to the air fryer.

Lightly spray all of the chicken with cooking oil. Air Fry for 15-16 minutes, shaking the basket once or until golden. Transfer chicken to a serving dish and drizzle with sweet chilli sauce. Serve immediately.

Easy Sage Chicken Thighs

Serves: 4 | Total Time: 30 minutes

INGREDIENTS

4 bone-in skinless chicken thighs
1 tbsp olive oil
1 tbsp lemon juice
3 tbsp cornflour

1 tsp dried sage
Black pepper to taste
20 garlic cloves, unpeeled

DIRECTIONS

Preheat your Air Fryer to 185°C. Brush the chicken with olive oil and lemon juice, then drizzle cornflour, sage, and pepper. Put the chicken in the frying basket and scatter the garlic cloves on top. Roast for 25 minutes or until the garlic is soft and the chicken is cooked through. Serve.

Curried Chicken Breasts

Serves: 4 | Total Time: 35 minutes + marinating time

INGREDIENTS

100g plain yogurt
2 tsp curry powder
2 garlic cloves, minced

1-cm piece ginger, grated
2 tsp olive oil
4 chicken breasts

DIRECTIONS

Mix the yogurt, curry powder, garlic, ginger, and olive oil in a bowl. Slice the chicken, without cutting, all the way through by making thin slits, then toss it into the yogurt mix. Coat well and let marinate for 10 minutes.

Preheat your Air Fryer to 180°C. Remove the chicken from the marinade, letting the extra liquid drip off. Toss the rest of the marinade away. Air Fry the chicken for 10 minutes. Turn each piece, then cook for 8-13 minutes more until cooked through and no pink meat remains. Serve warm.

Creamy Chicken Drumettes

Serves 4 | Total Time: 50 minutes

INGREDIENTS

500g chicken drumettes
Salt and pepper to taste
60g flour
60ml double cream

60ml sour cream
60g bread crumbs
2 tbsp olive oil

DIRECTIONS

Preheat your Air Fryer to 185°C. Season chicken drumettes with salt and pepper and coat them with. Shake away excess flour and set aside. Mix the double cream and sour cream in a bowl.

In another bowl, place the bread crumbs. Dip floured drumettes in cream mixture, then dredge them in crumbs. Place the chicken drumettes in the greased frying basket and Air Fry for 20 minutes, tossing once and brushing with melted butter. Let rest for a few minutes on a plate and serve.

Chicken Skewers

Serves: 4 | Total Time: 25 minutes

INGREDIENTS

1 green pepper, cut into chunks
1 red pepper, cut into chunks
4 chicken breasts, cubed

Salt and pepper to taste
16 cherry tomatoes
8 pearl onions, peeled

DIRECTIONS

Preheat your Air Fryer to 180°C. Season the cubes with salt and pepper. Thread metal skewers with chicken, pepper chunks, cherry tomatoes, and pearl onions.

Put the kabobs in the greased frying basket. Bake for 14-16 minutes, flipping once until cooked through. Let cool slightly. Serve.

Hawaiian Chicken

Serves: 4 | Total Time: 25 minutes

INGREDIENTS

450g tinned pineapple, diced
1 kiwi, sliced
2 tbsp coconut aminos

1 tbsp honey
Salt and pepper to taste
500g chicken breasts

DIRECTIONS

Preheat your Air Fryer to 180°C. Stir together pineapple, kiwi, coconut aminos, honey, salt, and pepper in a small bowl. Arrange the chicken in a single layer in a baking dish.

Spread half of the pineapple mixture over the top of the chicken. Transfer the dish to the basket. Roast for 8 minutes, then flip the chicken. Spread the rest of the pineapple mixture over the top of the chicken and Roast for another 8-10 until the chicken is done. Allow sitting for 5 minutes. Serve and enjoy!

Hot Mexican Chicken Wings

Serves 4 | Total Time: 35 minutes

INGREDIENTS

900g chicken wings, split at the joint
2 tbsp melted butter
2 tbsp grated Cotija cheese

4 cloves garlic, minced
½ tbsp hot paprika
¼ tsp salt

DIRECTIONS

Preheat your Air Fryer to 130°C. Coat the chicken wings with 1 tbsp of butter. Place them in the basket and Air Fry for 12 minutes, tossing once. In another bowl, whisk 1 tbsp of butter, Cotija cheese, garlic, hot paprika, and salt. Reserve.

Increase temperature to 200°C. Air Fry wings for 10 more minutes, tossing twice. Transfer them to the bowl with the sauce, and toss to coat. Serve immediately.

Minty Chicken Legs

Serves 4 | Total Time: 40 minutes

INGREDIENTS

100g Greek yogurt
1 tbsp tomato paste
½ tbsp oregano

1 tsp salt
700g chicken legs
2 tbsp chopped fresh mint

DIRECTIONS

Combine yogurt, tomato paste, oregano, and salt in a bowl. Divide the mixture in half. Cover one half and store it in the fridge. In the other half, toss in the chicken until coated and marinated, covering it in the refrigerator for 30 minutes up to overnight.

Preheat your Air Fryer to 185°C. Shake excess marinade from chicken. Place chicken legs in the greased frying basket and Air Fry for 18 minutes, flipping once and brushing with the yogurt mixture. Serve topped with mint.

Glazed Chicken Tenders

Serves 4 | Total Time: 20 minutes + marinating time

INGREDIENTS

500g chicken tenderloins
30g strawberry jam
3 tbsp chopped basil

1 tsp orange juice
½ tsp orange zest
Salt and pepper to taste

DIRECTIONS

Combine all ingredients, except basil, in a bowl. Marinade in the fridge covered for 30 minutes. Preheat your Air Fryer to 175°C. Place the chicken tenders in the frying basket and Air Fry for 4-6 minutes. Shake the basket gently and turn over the chicken. Cook for 5 more minutes. Top with basil and serve.

Basil Chicken Meatballs

Serves 4 | Total Time: 35 minutes

INGREDIENTS

40g cottage cheese crumbles
500g minced chicken
½ tsp onion powder

30g chopped basil
60g bread crumbs

DIRECTIONS

Preheat your Air Fryer to 175°C. Combine the minced chicken, onion, basil, cottage cheese, and bread crumbs in a bowl. Form into 18 meatballs, about 2 tbsp each. Place the chicken meatballs in the greased frying basket and Air Fry for 12 minutes, shaking once. Serve.

Za'atar Chicken Drumsticks

Serves: 4 | Total Time: 45 minutes

INGREDIENTS

2 tbsp butter, melted
8 chicken drumsticks
1 ½ tbsp Za'atar seasoning

Salt and pepper to taste
1 lemon, zested
2 tbsp parsley, chopped

DIRECTIONS

Preheat your Air Fryer to 195°C. Mix the Za'atar seasoning, lemon zest, parsley, salt, and pepper in a bowl. Add the chicken drumsticks and toss to coat. Place them in the air fryer and brush them with butter. Air Fry for 18-20 minutes, flipping once until crispy. Serve and enjoy!

Garlicky Chicken Thighs

Serves: 4 | Total Time: 35 minutes

INGREDIENTS

4 boneless, skinless chicken thighs
120ml salsa verde

1 tsp mashed garlic

DIRECTIONS

Preheat your Air Fryer to 175°C. Add chicken thighs to a cake pan and cover with salsa verde and garlic. Place the cake pan in the frying basket and Bake for 30 minutes. Serve.

Parmesan Chicken Tenders

Serves: 4 | Total Time: 25 minutes

INGREDIENTS

120g grated Parmesan cheese
30g grated cheddar cheese
600g chicken tenders

1 egg, beaten
2 tbsp milk
Salt and pepper to taste

DIRECTIONS

Preheat your Air Fryer to 200°C. Combine egg, milk, salt, and pepper in a bowl. Mix cheddar and Parmesan cheese on a plate. Dip the chicken in the egg mix, then in the cheese mix, and press to coat.

Lay the tenders in the frying basket in a single layer. Spray all with oil and Bake for 12-16 minutes, flipping once halfway through cooking.

Cranberry Chicken Biryani

Serves: 4 | Total Time: 30 minutes

INGREDIENTS

3 chicken breasts, cubed
2 tsp olive oil
2 tbsp cornflour

1 apple, chopped
40g dried cranberries
1 cooked basmati rice

DIRECTIONS

Preheat your Air Fryer to 190°C. Brush the chicken with olive oil, then coat it with cornflour. Transfer to a baking pan and add the apple. Put the pan in the air fryer and Bake for 8 minutes, stirring once.

Add ½ cup of water and cranberries and continue baking for 10 minutes, letting the sauce thicken. The chicken should be lightly charred and cooked through. Serve warm with basmati rice.

Italian Chicken Cheeseburgers

Serves 4 | Total Time: 40 minutes

INGREDIENTS

30g shredded Pepper Jack cheese
500g minced chicken
2 tbsp onion

1 egg white, beaten
1 tbsp pesto
Salt and pepper to taste

DIRECTIONS

Preheat your Air Fryer to 175°C. Combine minced chicken, onion, cheese, egg white, salt, and pepper in a bowl. Make 4 patties out of the mixture. Place them in the greased frying basket and Air Fry for 12-14 minutes until golden, flipping once. Serve topped with pesto.

Wrapped Chicken Tenders

Serves: 4 | Total Time: 35 minutes

INGREDIENTS

2 tbsp parsley, chopped
Salt and black pepper to taste

500g chicken tenders
8 bacon slices

DIRECTIONS

Preheat your Air Fryer to 185°C. Sprinkle the chicken tenders with salt, pepper, and parsley and wrap each one in a slice of bacon. Put the wrapped chicken in the frying basket in a single layer and Air Fry for 18-20 minutes, flipping once until the bacon is crisp. Serve with sauce.

Chicken Goujons

Serves 4 | Total Time: 25 minutes

INGREDIENTS

2 chicken breasts, cut into strips
60g crushed corn crackers (flakes)
3 tbsp flour

2 tsp olive oil
½ tsp lime pepper seasoning
3 egg whites, beaten

DIRECTIONS

Preheat your Air Fryer to 190°C. Rub the chicken strips with lime pepper seasoning, then dust them in the flour. Next, dip in the egg whites and coat in the corn flakes. Put onto the greased frying basket. Air Fry for 10-14 minutes, turning halfway through, until golden and crisp.

Parsley Chicken Breasts

Serves 4 | Total Time: 30 minutes

INGREDIENTS

2 chicken breasts, halved lengthwise
30g honey mustard
30g chopped pecans

1 tbsp olive oil
1 tbsp parsley, chopped

DIRECTIONS

Preheat your Air Fryer to 175°C. Brush chicken breasts with honey mustard and olive oil on all sides. Place the pecans in a bowl. Add and coat the chicken breasts. Place the breasts in the greased frying basket and Air Fry for 25 minutes, turning once. Let chill for 5 minutes. Sprinkle with parsley. Serve.

Chicken Kabobs

Serves 4 | Total Time: 35 minutes+ chilling time

INGREDIENTS

500g boneless, skinless chicken thighs, cubed
1 green pepper, chopped
60g honey mustard

½ yellow onion, chopped
8 cherry tomatoes

DIRECTIONS

Toss chicken cubes and honey mustard in a bowl and let chill covered in the fridge for 30 minutes. Preheat your Air Fryer to 175°C. Thread chicken cubes, onion, cherry tomatoes, and peppers, alternating, onto 8 skewers. Place them on a kebab rack. Place the rack in the frying basket and Air Fry for 12 minutes.

Sweet Chilli Chicken Strips

Serves: 2 | Total Time: 20 minutes

INGREDIENTS

450g chicken strips
150ml sweet chilli sauce

60g bread crumbs
60g cornmeal

DIRECTIONS

Preheat your Air Fryer to 175°C. Combine chicken strips and sweet chilli sauce in a bowl until fully coated. In another bowl, mix the remaining ingredients.

Dredge strips in the mixture. Shake off any excess. Place chicken strips in the greased frying basket and Air Fry for 10 minutes, tossing once. Serve.

Spinach Turkey Meatballs

Serves: 4 | Total Time: 45 minutes

INGREDIENTS

30g grated Parmesan cheese
1 egg, beaten
120g baby spinach

30g breadcrumbs
Salt and pepper to taste
600g minced turkey

DIRECTIONS

Preheat your Air Fryer to 200°C. Combine Parmesan cheese, egg, baby spinach, breadcrumbs, salt, and pepper in a bowl and mix well. Add the turkey and mix again, then form into 4-cm balls. Add the meatballs in the frying basket and Air Fry for 10-15 minutes, shaking once. Serve.

Turkey Quesadillas

Serves: 4 | Total Time: 15 minutes

INGREDIENTS

100g cooked turkey breast, pulled
6 tortilla wraps
40g grated Swiss cheese

1 small red onion, sliced
2 tbsp Mexican chilli sauce

DIRECTIONS

Preheat your Air Fryer to 200°C. Lay 3 tortilla wraps on a clean workspace, then spoon equal amounts of Swiss cheese, turkey, Mexican chilli sauce, and red onion on the tortillas.

Spritz the exterior of the tortillas with cooking spray. Air Fry the quesadillas, one at a time, for 5-8 minutes until crispy. Serve.

Cheesy Turkey Burgers

Serves: 4 | Total Time: 30 minutes

INGREDIENTS

2 tbsp finely grated Emmental cheese
40g minced onions
2 garlic cloves, minced

2 tsp olive oil
1 egg
500g minced turkey

DIRECTIONS

Preheat your Air Fryer to 200°C. Mix the onions, garlic, olive oil, Emmental cheese, minced turkey, and egg in a bowl. Use your hands to mix the ingredients. Form the mixture into 4 patties. Set them in the air fryer and Air Fry for 18-20 minutes, flipping once until cooked through and golden.

Turkey Scotch Eggs

Serves: 4 | Total Time: 30 minutes

INGREDIENTS

700g minced turkey
3 eggs
180g bread crumbs

6 hard-cooked eggs, peeled
60g flour

DIRECTIONS

Preheat your Air Fryer to 185°C. Place the turkey, one egg, and 60g of bread crumbs in a large bowl and mix until well incorporated. Divide into 4 equal portions, then flatten each into long ovals. Set aside.

In a shallow bowl, beat the remaining eggs. In another shallow bowl, add flour. Do the same with another plate for bread crumbs. Roll each cooked egg in flour, then wrap with one oval of chicken sausage until completely covered.

Roll again in flour, then coat in the beaten egg before rolling in bread crumbs. Arrange the eggs in the greased frying basket. Air Fry for 12-14 minutes, flipping once until the sausage is cooked and the eggs are brown. Serve.

Herby Turkey Breast

Serves: 6 | Total Time: 65 minutes

INGREDIENTS

3 tbsp olive oil
6 garlic cloves, minced
½ tsp dried thyme
½ tsp dried rosemary

Salt and pepper to taste
1 (1½-2 kg) bone-in turkey breast
1 tbsp chopped coriander

DIRECTIONS

Preheat your Air Fryer to 180°C. Pat the turkey breast dry with paper towels. Combine olive oil, garlic, thyme, rosemary, salt, and pepper in a small bowl.

Rub the seasoning mixture all over the turkey breast, making sure to coat it evenly. Place the seasoned turkey breast in the Air Fryer basket.

Air Fry the turkey breast for 25-30 minutes, flipping halfway through the cooking time, until the internal temperature reaches 75°C and the outside is golden brown and crispy. Remove the turkey breast from the Air Fryer and let it rest for 5-7 minutes before slicing. Serve sprinkled with coriander.

Asian Turkey Meatballs

Serves: 4 | Total Time: 25 minutes

INGREDIENTS

30g panko bread crumbs
500g minced turkey
½ tsp ground ginger

1 tbsp olive oil
1 small onion, minced
1 egg, beaten

DIRECTIONS

Preheat your Air Fryer to 200°C. Place the minced turkey, ginger, onion, egg, and bread crumbs in a bowl and stir to combine. Form the turkey mixture into 2-cm meatballs. Arrange the meatballs in the baking pan. Drizzle with sesame oil. Bake until the meatballs are cooked through, 10-12 minutes, flipping once.

Sage Turkey

Serves: 4 | Total Time: 35 minutes

INGREDIENTS

2 turkey tenderloins
2 tbsp olive oil

Salt and pepper to taste
1 tbsp minced sage

DIRECTIONS

Preheat your Air Fryer to 175°C. Brush the tenderloins with oil and sprinkle with sage, salt, and pepper. Put the tenderloins in the frying basket and Bake for 22-27 minutes, flipping once until cooked through. Let stand the turkey for 5 minutes. Slice before serving.

Tyrkey Tortilla Chips

Serves: 4 | Total Time: 25 minutes

INGREDIENTS

½ cup salsa
2 cups cooked turkey, shredded
170g lightly salted tortilla chips

1 (400g) tin black beans, drained
2 cups mozzarella cheese, shredded

DIRECTIONS

Preheat your Air Fryer to 190°C. Coat the cooked turkey with salsa in a bowl. Spread half of the tortilla chips evenly on a gresaed baking dish. Layer half of the turkey and salsa mixture over the tortilla chips.

Add half of the black beans. Sprinkle half of the mozzarella cheese over the beans. Repeat the layers with the remaining tortilla chips, turkey and salsa mixture, black beans, and mozzarella cheese.

Place the assembled chips in the Air Fryer. Air fry for about 8-10 minutes or until the cheese is melted and bubbly. Once cooked, remove the chips from the Air Fryer and let them cool slightly before serving.

FISH AND SEAFOOD

Lemony Salmon

Serves: 4 | Total Time: 30 minutes

INGREDIENTS

4 salmon fillets
2 eggs, beaten
2 tbsp olive oil
1 garlic clove, minced

1 tsp lemon zest
Salt and pepper to taste
60g peanuts, crushed

DIRECTIONS

Preheat your Air Fryer to 175°C. Put the beaten eggs, olive oil, lemon zest, garlic, salt, and pepper in a bowl and stir thoroughly. Dip in the salmon fillets, then roll them in the crushed peanuts, coating them completely. Place the coated salmon fillets in the frying basket. Air Fry for 14-16 minutes, flipping halfway through cooking until the salmon crust is toasted and crispy. Serve.

Cod and Collard Green Packets

Serves: 4 | Total Time: 20 minutes

INGREDIENTS

200g collard greens, chopped
1 tsp salt
½ tsp garlic powder
4 cod fillets

1 shallot, thinly sliced
50ml olive oil
1 lemon, juiced

DIRECTIONS

Preheat your Air Fryer to 190°C. Rub the garlic powder and salt onto the cod fillets. Divide them among 4 sheets of foil. Top with shallot slices and collard greens. Drizzle with olive oil and lemon juice. Fold and seal the sides of the foil packets and then place them into the frying basket. Steam in the fryer for 11-13 minutes until the cod is cooked through. Serve and enjoy!

Basil-Crusted Salmon

Serves: 4 | Total Time: 20 minutes

INGREDIENTS

40g crushed potato chips
4 skinless salmon fillets
3 tbsp honey mustard

½ tsp dried basil
30g panko breadcrumbs
2 tbsp olive oil

DIRECTIONS

Preheat your Air Fryer to 160°C.Place the salmon on a work surface. Mix mustard and basil in a small bowl. Spread on top of the salmon evenly. Mix bread crumbs and potato chips in a separate small bowl before drizzling with olive oil. Place the salmon in the frying basket. Bake until the salmon is cooked, and the topping is crispy and brown, about 10 minutes. Serve.

Dilly Salmon

Serves: 4 | Total Time: 15 minutes

INGREDIENTS

2 tbsp olive oil
4 salmon fillets
½ tsp salt
1 tsp chopped dill

2 tomatoes, diced
50g sliced black olives
4 lemon slices

DIRECTIONS

Preheat your Air Fryer to 190°C. Lightly brush the olive oil on both sides of the salmon fillets and season them with salt and dill. Put the fillets in a single layer in the frying basket, then layer the tomatoes and black olives over the top. Top each fillet with a lemon slice. Bake for 8 minutes. Serve and enjoy!

Roasted Red Pepper and Cod Roulades

Serves: 4 | Total Time: 25 minutes

INGREDIENTS

4 jarred roasted red pepper slices
1 egg
60g breadcrumbs
Salt and pepper to taste

4 cod fillets
2 tbsp olive oil
4 lime wedges

DIRECTIONS

Preheat your Air Fryer to 175°C. Beat the egg and 2 tbsp of water in a bowl. Mix the breadcrumbs, salt, and pepper in another bowl. Top the cod fillets with red pepper slices. Tightly roll cod fillets from one short end to the other. Secure with toothpicks. Roll each fillet in the egg mixture.

Dredge them in the breadcrumbs. Place the fish rolls in the greased basket. Drizzle the tops with olive oil. Roast for 6 minutes. Let rest for 5 minutes before removing the toothpicks. Serve with lime wedges.

Chilli Tuna with Coriander

Serves: 4 | Total Time: 20 minutes

INGREDIENTS

2 tbsp olive oil
2 garlic cloves, minced
Salt and pepper to taste
¼ tsp chilli powder

¼ tsp lemon zest
1 tbsp chopped coriander
4 tuna fillets

DIRECTIONS

Preheat your Air Fryer to 165°C. Combine olive oil, garlic, salt, pepper, lemon zest, and chilli powder in a small bowl. Place the tuna on a large plate, then spread the seasoned butter on top of each.

Arrange the fish fillets in a single layer on the parchment-lined frying basket. Bake for 6 minutes, then carefully flip the fish. Bake for another 6-7 minutes until the fish is flaky and cooked. Serve sprinkled with coriander. Enjoy!

Air Fryer Fish 'n' Chips

Serves: 4 | Total Time: 40 minutes

INGREDIENTS

2 russet potatoes, peeled
2 tbsp olive oil
4 cod fillets
30g plain flour

Salt and pepper to taste
1 egg, beaten
120g panko breadcrumbs

DIRECTIONS

Preheat the air fryer to 200°C. Slice the potatoes into 1-cm-thick chips and drizzle with olive oil. Sprinkle with salt. Add the fries to the frying basket and Air Fry for 12-16 minutes, shaking once.

Remove the potatoes to a plate. Cover loosely with foil to keep warm. Sprinkle the fish with salt and pepper. Dip the fish in the flour, egg, and panko. Press to coat thoroughly. Add the fish to the frying basket and spray with cooking oil. Air Fry for 8-10 minutes until the fish flakes. Serve.

Garam Masala Fish with Potato Wedges

Serves: 4 | Total Time: 40 minutes

INGREDIENTS

700g russet potatoes, peeled and cut into wedges
4 cod fillets
Salt and pepper to taste
1 tsp garam masala

1 egg white
100g bread crumbs
2 tbsp olive oil

DIRECTIONS

Preheat your Air Fryer to 200°C. In a bowl, toss the potato wedges with olive oil, salt, and pepper. Place them in the frying basket and Air Fry for 18-20 minutes, shaking once. Remove them and cover with foil to keep warm. Coat the cod fillets with salt, pepper, and garam masala.

In a bowl, whisk the egg white until frothy. Add the bread crumbs to a separate bowl. Dip the fillets into the egg white, then coat with bread crumbs. Arrange the fish fillets on the frying basket and cook them for 8-10 minutes, flipping once. Add the chops back to the basket and cook until heated through, 2 minutes. Serve warm.

Chilli Flaming Haddock

Serves 2 | Total Time: 20 minutes

INGREDIENTS

2 tbsp butter, melted
½ tsp chilli powder

60g bread crumbs
2 haddock fillets

DIRECTIONS

Preheat your Air Fryer to 175°C. In a bowl, mix the butter, chilli powder, and bread crumbs. Press the mixture onto the tops of haddock fillets. Place haddock in the greased frying basket and Air Fry for 10 minutes or until the fish is opaque and flakes easily with a fork. Serve right away.

Wine Salmon with Green Beans

Serves: 4 | Total Time: 20 minutes

INGREDIENTS

2 tbsp olive oil
4 garlic cloves, minced
30ml white wine
Salt and pepper to taste

4 wild-caught salmon fillets
20 halved cherry tomatoes
500g green beans, trimmed

DIRECTIONS

Preheat your Air Fryer to 185°C. Combine olive oil, garlic, wine, salt, and pepper in a small bowl. Spread the mixture over the top of the salmon. Arrange the fillets on the frying basket.

Surround the fish with green beans and cherry tomatoes. Bake for 12-15 minutes until salmon is cooked and vegetables are tender. Serve and enjoy!

Pesto-Coated Cod

Serves 4 | Total Time: 25 minutes

INGREDIENTS

1 egg
2 tbsp buttermilk
4 cod fillets
100g crushed cornflakes

Salt and pepper to taste
4 tsp pesto
2 tbsp olive oil

DIRECTIONS

Preheat your Air Fryer to 175°C. Whisk egg and buttermilk in a bowl. In another bowl, combine cornflakes, salt, and pepper. Spread 1 tsp of pesto on each cod fillet, then tightly roll the fillet from one short end to the other. Secure with a toothpick.

Dip each fillet in the egg mixture and dredge in the cornflake mixture. Place fillets in the greased frying basket, drizzle with olive oil, and Air Fry for 6 minutes. Let rest on a serving dish for 5 minutes before removing the toothpicks. Serve.

Sicilian-Inspired Mackerel

Serves: 4 | Total Time: 20 minutes

INGREDIENTS

4 mackerel fillets
Salt to taste
3 garlic cloves, minced
1 tomato, sliced

50g sliced Sicilian olives
1 lemon, juiced
2 tbsp olive oil

DIRECTIONS

Preheat your Air Fryer to 190°C. Sprinkle the mackerel fillets with salt. Arrange them on the greased frying basket and top with garlic, tomato slices, and olives. Drizzle with lemon juice and olive oil. Bake for 10-12 minutes. Serve and enjoy!

French-Style Sea Bass Fillets

Serves: 4 | Total Time: 30 minutes

INGREDIENTS

60g hazelnuts, ground
1 spring onion, finely chopped
1 lemon, juiced and zested
½ tbsp olive oil

Salt and pepper to taste
3 skinless sea bass fillets
1 tsp Dijon mustard

DIRECTIONS

Place the hazelnuts in a small bowl with green onion, lemon zest, olive oil, salt, and pepper. Mix everything until combined. Spray only the top of the fish with cooking oil, then squeeze lemon juice onto the fish. Coat the top of the fish with mustard. Spread with hazelnuts and press gently.

Preheat your Air Fryer to 165°C. Air Fry the fish in the greased frying basket for 7-8 minutes or until it starts browning and the fish is cooked through. Serve hot.

Rice Flour-Breaded Cod Goujons

Serves: 2 | Total Time: 30 minutes

INGREDIENTS

1 cod fillet, cut into chunks
2 eggs, beaten
30g breadcrumbs

30g rice flour
1 tsp dried dill
Salt and pepper to taste

DIRECTIONS

Preheat your Air Fryer to 175°C. In a bowl, mix the breadcrumbs, rice flour, dill, salt, and pepper. Dip the cod chunks in the beaten eggs, then coat them with the crumb mixture.

Transfer the coated cod to the greased frying basket. Air Fry for 14-16 minutes until the fish goujons are cooked through and their crust is golden, brown, and delicious. Toss the basket two or three times during the cooking time. Serve.

Cayenne Pepper Ahi Tuna Steaks

Serves: 4 | Total Time: 15 minutes

INGREDIENTS

1 tsp garlic powder
Salt to taste
¼ tsp dried thyme
¼ tsp cayenne pepper

4 ahi tuna steaks
2 tbsp olive oil
1 lemon, cut into wedges

DIRECTIONS

Preheat your Air Fryer to 190°C. SMix the garlic powder, salt, thyme, and cayenne pepper in a bowl. Coat the tuna steaks with olive oil. Season both sides of each steak with the seasoning mix. Put the steaks in the frying basket. Air Fry for 5 minutes, then flip and cook for 3-4 minutes. Serve warm with lemon wedges on the side.

Haddock Strips with Tartar Sauce

Serves: 4 | Total Time: 20 minutes

INGREDIENTS

30g plain flour
Salt and pepper to taste
1 egg

4 haddock fillets
1 lemon, thinly sliced
60ml tartar sauce

DIRECTIONS

Preheat your Air Fryer to 200°C. Combine flour, salt, and pepper in a wide bowl. Whisk egg and 1 teaspoon water in another wide bowl. Slice each fillet into 4 strips. Dip the strips in the egg mixture. Then, roll them in the flour mixture and coat completely.

Arrange the fish strips on the greased frying basket. Air Fry for 4 minutes. Flip the fish and Air Fry for another 4 to 5 minutes until crisp. Serve warm with lemon slices and tartar sauce on the side and enjoy.

Parmesan Fish Bites

Serves: 2 | Total Time: 30 minutes

INGREDIENTS

1 haddock fillet, cut into bite-sized pieces
3 tbsp shredded Parmesan cheese
½ tsp dried thyme
2 eggs, beaten

60g breadcrumbs
Salt and pepper to taste

DIRECTIONS

Preheat your Air Fryer to 175°C. Dip the strips in the beaten eggs. Mix the bread crumbs, Parmesan cheese, thyme, salt, and pepper in a bowl. Coat the fish strips in the dry mixture and place them on the foil-lined frying basket.

Air Fry for 14-16 minutes. Halfway through the cooking time, shake the basket. When the cooking time is over, the fish will be cooked through and crust golden brown. Serve and enjoy!

Stuffed Tomatoes with Seafood

Serves 4 | Total Time: 25 minutes

INGREDIENTS

4 medium tomatoes, top removed
120g lump crabmeat, shells discarded
1 tsp lemon juice
Salt and pepper to taste

2 tbsp bread crumbs
2 tbsp olive oil
2 tbsp grated Parmesan cheese

DIRECTIONS

Preheat your Air Fryer to 175°C. Scoop out the pulp of the tomatoes. Chop the pulp and place it in a bowl. Mix well with the crabmeat, lemon juice, salt, and pepper. Fill the tomatoes with crab stuffing, scatter bread crumbs over, and drizzle olive oil over the crumbs. Place the stuffed tomatoes in the frying basket. Sprinkle with Parmesan cheese and Bake for 10-15 minutes. Serve.

Paprika Fish Sticks

Serves: 4 | Total Time: 30 minutes

INGREDIENTS

500g cod fillets, cut into sticks
120g plain flour
1 egg

30g cornmeal
Salt and pepper to taste
¼ tsp smoked paprika

DIRECTIONS

Preheat your Air Fryer to 175°C. In a bowl, add half of the flour. In another bowl, beat the egg, and in a third bowl, combine the remaining flour, cornmeal, salt, black pepper, and paprika.

Roll the sticks in the flour and shake off excess flour. Then, dip them in the egg. Finally, dredge them in the cornmeal mixture. Place fish fingers in the greased frying basket and Air Fry for 10 minutes, flipping once. Serve and enjoy!

Almond Lemon Trout

Serves: 4 | Total Time: 20 minutes

INGREDIENTS

4 trout fillets
2 tbsp olive oil
Salt and pepper to taste

2 garlic cloves, sliced
1 lemon, sliced
1 tbsp flaked almonds

DIRECTIONS

Preheat your Air Fryer to 190°C. Lightly brush each fillet with olive oil and season with salt and pepper. Put the fillets in a single layer in the frying basket. Put the sliced garlic over the tops of the trout fillets, then top with lemon slices and cook for 12-15 minutes. Serve topped with flaked almonds. Enjoy!

Sardines with Romesco Sauce

Serves 2 | Total Time: 15 minutes

INGREDIENTS

2x100g tins skinless, boneless sardines in oil, drained
100ml warmed romesco sauce

60g bread crumbs

DIRECTIONS

Preheat your Air Fryer to 175°C. In a shallow dish, add bread crumbs. Roll in sardines to coat. Place sardines in the greased frying basket and Air Fry for 6 minutes, turning once. Serve with romesco sauce.

Prawns with Pesto

Serves: 4 | Total Time: 10 minutes

INGREDIENTS

500g peeled prawns, deveined
50ml pesto sauce

1 lime, sliced
250g cooked farro

DIRECTIONS

Preheat your Air Fryer to 180°C. Coat the prawns with the pesto sauce in a bowl. Put the prawns in a single layer in the frying basket. Put the lime slices over the prawns and Roast for 5 minutes. Remove lime and discard. Serve the prawns over a bed of farro pilaf. Enjoy!

Lime Salmon Croquettes

Serves: 6 | Total Time: 20 minutes

INGREDIENTS

450g tinned Alaskan pink salmon, bones removed
1 lime, zested
1 egg, beaten
60g bread crumbs

2 scallions, diced
Salt and pepper to taste

DIRECTIONS

Preheat your Air Fryer to 200°C. Mix salmon, beaten egg, and bread crumbs in a large bowl. Add lime, salt, and pepper. Divide into 6 even portions and shape into patties. Place them in the greased frying basket and Air Fry for 7 minutes. Flip them and cook for 4 minutes or until golden.

Tuna Tacos

Serves: 4 | Total Time: 20 minutes

INGREDIENTS

500g fresh tuna steak, cubed
2 garlic cloves, minced
½ tsp olive oil

4 tortillas
30ml mild salsa
1 red pepper, sliced

DIRECTIONS

Preheat your Air Fryer to 185°C. Combine tuna, garlic, and olive oil in a bowl and allow them to marinate for 10 minutes. Lay the marinated tuna in the fryer and Grill for 4-7 minutes. Serve right away with tortillas, mild salsa, and red pepper slices.

Asian Salmon

Serves: 4 | Total Time: 20 minutes

INGREDIENTS

40ml honey
4 garlic cloves, minced
1 tbsp olive oil
½ tsp salt

½ tsp soy sauce
¼ tsp blackening seasoning
4 salmon fillets

DIRECTIONS

Preheat your Air Fryer to 190°C. Combine the honey, garlic, olive oil, soy sauce, blackening seasoning and salt in a bowl. Put the salmon in a single layer on the greased frying basket. Brush the top of each fillet with the honey-garlic mixture. Roast for 10-12 minutes. Serve and enjoy!

Tarragon Cod Fillets

Serves: 2 | Total Time: 20 minutes

INGREDIENTS

60g crushed potato chips
1 tsp chopped tarragon
Salt to taste
1 tbsp Dijon mustard

30ml buttermilk
1 tbsp olive oil
2 cod fillets

DIRECTIONS

Preheat your Air Fryer to 175°C. Mix all ingredients except cod fillets in a bowl. Press the mixture evenly across the tops of the cod. Place cod fillets in the greased frying basket and Air Fry for 10 minutes until the fish is opaque and flakes easily. Serve immediately.

Garlic-Lemon Scallops

Serves 2 | Total Time: 15 minutes

INGREDIENTS

2 tbsp butter, melted
1 garlic clove, minced

1 tbsp lemon juice
500g jumbo sea scallops

DIRECTIONS

Preheat your Air Fryer to 200°C. Whisk butter, garlic, and lemon juice in a bowl. Roll scallops in the mixture to coat all sides. Place scallops in the frying basket and Air Fry for 4 minutes, flipping once. Brush the tops of each scallop with butter mixture and cook for 4 more minutes, flipping once. Serve.

Hot Prawns

Serves 2 | Total Time: 15 minutes

INGREDIENTS

500g tail-on prawns, deveined
2 tbsp butter, melted

1 lemon wedge
½ red chilli, thinly sliced

DIRECTIONS

Preheat your Air Fryer to 180°C. Combine prawns and butter in a bowl. Place prawns in the greased frying basket and Air Fry for 6 minutes, flipping once. Squeeze lemon juice over and top with chilli slices. Serve warm and enjoy!

Fried Sardinas

Serves: 2 | Total Time: 15 minutes

INGREDIENTS

2 (100-g) tins boneless, skinless sardines in mustard sauce
Salt and pepper to taste
60g bread crumbs

2 lemon wedges
1 tsp chopped parsley

DIRECTIONS

Preheat your Air Fryer to 175°C. Add breadcrumbs, salt, and black pepper to a bowl. Roll sardines in the breadcrumbs to coat. Place them in the greased frying basket and Air Fry for 6 minutes, flipping once. Transfer them to a serving dish. Serve topped with parsley and lemon wedges.

Chilli Sea Bass

Serves 2 | Total Time: 15 minutes

INGREDIENTS

1 tbsp olive oil
¼ tsp chilli powder
2 cloves garlic, minced
1 tbsp lemon juice

¼ tsp salt
2 sea bass fillets
2 tsp chopped coriander

DIRECTIONS

Preheat your Air Fryer to 165°C. Whisk the butter, chilli powder, garlic, lemon juice, and salt in a bowl. Rub the mixture over the tops of each fillet. Place the fillets in the frying basket and Air Fry for 7 minutes. Let rest for 5 minutes. Divide between 2 plates and garnish with coriander to serve.

Dijon Cod Fillets

Serves 2 | Total Time: 20 minutes

INGREDIENTS

1 lemon wedge, juiced and zested
60g panko breadcrumbs
Salt to taste

1 tbsp Dijon mustard
1 tbsp butter, melted
2 cod fillets

DIRECTIONS

Preheat your Air Fryer to 175°C. Combine all ingredients, except fish, in a bowl. Press the mixture evenly across the tops of the cod fillets. Place fillets in the greased frying basket and Air Fry for 10 minutes until the cod is opaque and flakes easily with a fork. Serve immediately.

Rich Fish Nuggets

Serves 4 | Total Time: 30 minutes

INGREDIENTS

Salt and pepper to taste
1 egg, beaten
30g cornflour

30g plain flour
500g cod, cut into sticks

DIRECTIONS

Preheat your Air Fryer to 175°C. In a bowl, combine cornflour, flour, salt, and pepper. Dip fish nuggets in the beaten egg and roll them in the flour mixture. Place fish nuggets in the lightly greased frying basket and Air Fry for 10 minutes, flipping once. Serve with the sauce on the side.

Gochujang Fried Calamari

Serves 4 | Total Time: 25 minutes

INGREDIENTS

2 tbsp tomato paste
1 tbsp gochujang
1 tbsp lime juice

½ tsp salt
120g breadcrumbs
150g calamari rings

DIRECTIONS

Preheat your Air Fryer to 200°C. Whisk tomato paste, gochujang, lime juice, and salt in a bowl. Dredge calamari rings in the tomato mixture, shake off excess, then roll through the crumbs. Place calamari in the greased frying basket. Air Fry for 4-5 minutes, flipping once. Serve.

Tasty Bay Scallops

Serves 4 | Total Time: 10 minutes

INGREDIENTS

2 tbsp butter, melted
1 lime, juiced
¼ tsp salt

500g bay scallops
2 tbsp chopped coriander

DIRECTIONS

Preheat your Air Fryer to 175°C. Combine all ingredients in a bowl except for the coriander. Place scallops in the frying basket and Air Fry for 5 minutes, tossing once. Serve topped with coriander.

Fiery Prawns

Serves: 2 | Total Time: 15 minutes

INGREDIENTS

500g shelled tail-on prawns, deveined
2 tsp grated Parmesan cheese
2 tbsp olive oil
1 tsp cayenne pepper

1 tsp garlic powder
1 tbsp lemon juice

DIRECTIONS

Preheat your Air Fryer to 175°C. Toss the prawns, olive oil, cayenne pepper, and garlic powder in a bowl. Place them in the greased frying basket and Air Fry for 6 minutes, flipping once. Transfer it to a plate. Squeeze lemon juice over prawns and stir in Parmesan cheese. Serve immediately.

Garlic Mussels

Serves 2 | Total Time: 30 minutes

INGREDIENTS

1 kg mussels, cleaned and debearded
2 tbsp butter, melted

1 garlic clove, minced
2 lemon wedges

DIRECTIONS

Preheat your Air Fryer to 190°C. Place the mussels in the air fryer basket and Air Fry them for 8-10 minutes, shaking the basket halfway through cooking. Discard any mussels that remain closed. Once cooked, transfer the mussels to a serving dish. Drizzle with melted butter, garlic, and squeeze lemon on top.

Chilli Calamari Rings

Serves: 4 | Total Time: 25 minutes

INGREDIENTS

120g breadcrumbs
Salt and pepper to taste
60g plain flour

2 tsp hot chilli powder
2 eggs
500g calamari rings

DIRECTIONS

Preheat your Air Fryer to 200°C. In a bowl, mix the breadcrumbs, salt, and pepper. In another bowl, whisk the eggs. Dip calamari rings in flour mix first, then in egg mix, and shake off excess. Then, roll the calamari rings through the breadcrumb mixture. Place calamari rings in the greased frying basket and Air Fry for 4 minutes, tossing once. Squeeze lime quarters over calamari. Serve.

Coconut Prawns with Plum Sauce

Serves: 2 | Total Time: 30 minutes

INGREDIENTS

200g raw prawns, peeled
2 eggs
60g breadcrumbs

2 tbsp dried coconut flakes
Salt and pepper to taste
60ml plum sauce

DIRECTIONS

Preheat your Air Fryer to 175°C. Whisk the eggs with salt and pepper in a bowl. Dip in the prawns, fully submerging. Combine the bread crumbs, coconut flakes, salt, and pepper in another bowl until evenly blended. Coat the prawns in the crumb mixture and place them in the foil-lined frying basket. Air Fry for 14-16 minutes. Halfway through the cooking time, shake the basket. Serve with plum sauce.

Old Bay Lobster Tails

Serves 2 | Total Time: 20 minutes

INGREDIENTS

2 lobster tails
1 tbsp butter, melted
½ tsp Old Bay Seasoning

½ tsp garlic powder
2 lemon wedges

DIRECTIONS

Preheat your Air Fryer to 200°C. Using kitchen shears, cut down the middle of each lobster tail on the softer side. Carefully run your finger between the lobster meat and the shell to loosen the meat. Place lobster tails in the frying basket, cut sides up, and Air Fry for 4 minutes. Rub with butter, garlic powder, and Old Bay seasoning and cook for 4 more minutes. Garnish with lemon wedges. Serve and enjoy!

PORK, BEEF, AND LAMB

Smoked Paprika Pork Escalopes

Serves: 4 | Total Time: 45 minutes

INGREDIENTS

120g breadcrumbs
½ tsp thyme, chopped
½ tsp smoked paprika

4 pork loin chops
2 eggs, beaten
Salt and pepper to taste

DIRECTIONS

Preheat your Air Fryer to 180°C. Mix the breadcrumbs, thyme, smoked paprika, salt, and pepper in a bowl. Add the pork chops and toss to coat. Dip in the beaten eggs, then dip again into the dry ingredients. Place the coated chops in the greased frying basket and Air Fry for 16-18 minutes, turning once. Serve and enjoy!

Mexican-Style Pork Loin Chops

Serves: 4 | Total Time: 25 minutes

INGREDIENTS

8 thin boneless pork loin chops
¾ tsp salt
1 egg, beaten

1 tsp fajita seasoning
60g bread crumbs

DIRECTIONS

Place the chops between two sheets of parchment paper. Pound the pork to 0.5-cm thickness using a meat mallet or rolling pin. Season with salt. In a shallow bowl, beat the egg with 1 tsp of water and fajita seasoning. In a second bowl, pour the breadcrumbs. Dip the chops into the egg mixture, shake, and dip into the crumbs.

Preheat your Air Fryer to 200°C. Place the chops in the greased frying basket and Air Fry for 6-8 minutes, flipping once until golden and cooked through. Serve immediately.

Greek Pork Chops

Serves: 4 | Total Time: 30 minutes

INGREDIENTS

3 tbsp grated Halloumi cheese
4 pork chops
1 tsp Greek seasoning

Salt and pepper to taste
40g plain flour
2 tbsp bread crumbs

DIRECTIONS

Preheat your Air Fryer to 190°C. Season the pork chops with Greek seasoning, salt, and pepper. In a shallow bowl, add flour. In another shallow bowl, combine the crumbs and Halloumi. Dip the chops in the flour, then in the bread crumbs. Place them in the fryer and spray with cooking oil. Bake for 12-14 minutes, flipping once. Serve warm.

Wasabi Pork Medallions

Serves: 4 | Total Time: 20 minutes + marinate time

INGREDIENTS

500g pork medallions
2 tbsp soy sauce
1 tbsp mirin

60 ml olive oil
1 tsp fresh grated ginger
1 tsp wasabi paste

DIRECTIONS

Place all ingredients, except pork, in a resealable bag and shake to combine. Add the pork medallions to the bag, shake again, and place in the fridge to marinate for 2 hours.

Preheat your Air Fryer to 180°C. Remove pork medallions from the marinade and place them in the frying basket in rows. Air Fry for 14-16 minutes or until the medallions are cooked through and juicy.

Stuffed Pork Loins

Serves: 3 | Total Time: 25 minutes

INGREDIENTS

3 boneless center-cut pork loins, pocket cut in each loin
60g diced white mushrooms
1 tsp olive oil

3 bacon slices, diced
½ onion, peeled and diced
100g baby spinach
Salt and pepper to taste

DIRECTIONS

Warm the oil in a skillet over medium heat. Add the bacon and cook for 3 minutes until the fat is rendered but not crispy. Add onion and mushrooms and stir-fry for 3 minutes until the onions are translucent. Stir in spinach, salt, and pepper and cook for 1 minute until the spinach wilts. Set aside.

Preheat your Air Fryer to 175°C. Stuff spinach mixture into each pork loin. Place them in the frying basket and Air Fry for 14-16 minutes. Let rest on a cutting board for 5 minutes before serving.

Garlic Pork Tenderloin

Serves: 4 | Total Time: 25 minutes

INGREDIENTS

½ tsp dried tarragon
500g pork tenderloin, sliced
Salt and pepper to taste
2 tbsp Dijon mustard

1 garlic clove, minced
120g bread crumbs
2 tbsp olive oil

DIRECTIONS

Preheat your Air Fryer to 195°C. Using a rolling pin, pound the pork slices until they are about 2-cm thick. Season both sides with salt and pepper. Coat the pork with mustard, garlic, and tarragon.

In a shallow bowl, mix bread crumbs and olive oil. Dredge the pork with the bread crumbs, pressing firmly so that it adheres. Put the pork in the frying basket and Air Fry until the pork outside is brown and crisp, 12-14 minutes. Serve warm.

Pork Escalopes

Serves: 4 | Total Time: 20 minutes

INGREDIENTS

4 pork loin steaks
Salt and pepper to taste

40g flour
2 tbsp bread crumbs

DIRECTIONS

Preheat your Air Fryer to 190°C. Season pork with salt and pepper. In one shallow bowl, add flour. In another, add bread crumbs. Dip the steaks first in the flour, then in the crumbs. Place them in the fryer and spray with oil. Bake for 12-14 minutes, flipping once until crisp. Serve.

Home-Style Teriyaki Pork Ribs

Serves: 4 | Total Time: 30 minutes

INGREDIENTS

1 ½ kg rack ribs, cut into individual bones
3 tbsp teriyaki sauce
2 tbsp honey
3 tbsp ketchup

Black pepper to taste
1 tsp ginger powder

DIRECTIONS

Preheat your Air Fryer to 190°C. Toss the ribs with all the ingredients in a baking pan that fits in the fryer to coat. Air Fry for 14-18 minutes, flipping once. Serve.

Apple and Celery Pork Tenderloin

Serves: 4 | Total Time: 30 minutes

INGREDIENTS

500g pork tenderloin, cut into 4 pieces
2 Granny Smith apples, sliced
3 tsp olive oil
3 celery stalks, sliced

1 onion, sliced
50 ml apple juice

DIRECTIONS

Preheat your Air Fryer to 200°C. Brush olive oil over the pork, then toss the pork, apples, celery, onion, and apple juice in a baking pan. Put the pan in the air fryer and Roast for 15-19 minutes until the pork is cooked through and the apples and veggies are soft, stirring once during cooking. Serve warm.

Mini Pork Meatballs

Serves 4 | Total Time: 35 minutes

INGREDIENTS

500g minced pork
1 egg
30g chipotle sauce

2 tbsp chopped coriander
30g plain flour
¼ tsp salt

DIRECTIONS

Preheat your Air Fryer to 175°C. In a large bowl, combine the minced pork, egg, chipotle sauce, coriander, flour, and salt. Form the mixture into 16 meatballs. Place the meatballs in the lightly greased frying basket and Air Fry for 8-10 minutes, flipping once. Serve immediately

Ginger Honey Pork Loin

Serves: 6 | Total Time: 25 minutes

INGREDIENTS

Salt and black pepper to taste
2 tbsp soy sauce
2 tbsp honey
1 tbsp olive oil

¼ tsp ground ginger
2 cloves garlic, minced
1 kg boneless pork loin

DIRECTIONS

Preheat your Air Fryer to 200°C. Mix all ingredients in a bowl. Massage the mixture into all sides of the pork loin. Place the seasoned pork in the greased frying basket and Roast for 14-18 minutes, flipping once. Let rest on a cutting board for 5 minutes before slicing. Serve right away.

French Pork Roast

Serves 4 | Total Time: 50 minutes

INGREDIENTS

1 (1 kg) boneless pork loin roast
2 tbsp Dijon mustard
2 tsp olive oil
1 tsp honey

1 garlic clove, minced
Salt and pepper to taste
1 tsp dried rosemary

DIRECTIONS

Preheat your Air Fryer to 175°C. Whisk all ingredients in a bowl. Massage into loin on all sides. Place the loin in the frying basket and Roast for 40 minutes, turning once. Let sit for 5 minutes before slicing.

Tamari Pork Strips

Serves: 4 | Total Time: 30 minutes + chilling time

INGREDIENTS

70 ml lemon juice
2 tbsp lemon marmalade
1 tbsp olive oil

2 tbsp tamari
1 tsp yellow mustard
500g pork shoulder strips

DIRECTIONS

Whisk the lemon juice, lemon marmalade, olive oil, tamari, and mustard in a bowl. Reserve half of the marinade. Toss pork strips with half of the marinade and let marinate in the fridge for 30 minutes.

Preheat your Air Fryer to 175°C. Place pork strips in the frying basket and Air Fry for 17 minutes, tossing twice. Transfer them to a bowl and stir in the remaining marinade. Serve.

Jalapeño Beef Patties

Serves: 2 | Total Time: 30 minutes

INGREDIENTS

200g minced beef
1 ½ tbsp ketchup
1 ½ tbsp tamari

½ tsp jalapeño powder
½ tsp mustard powder
Salt and pepper to taste

DIRECTIONS

Preheat your Air Fryer to 180°C. Add the beef, ketchup, tamari, jalapeño, mustard salt, and pepper to a bowl and mix until evenly combined. Shape into 2 patties, then place them on the greased frying basket. Air Fry for 18-20 minutes, turning once. Serve and enjoy!

Homemade Beef Fajitas

Serves 2 | Total Time: 15 minutes

INGREDIENTS

250g sliced mushrooms
½ onion, cut into half-moons
1 tbsp olive oil
Salt and pepper to taste

1 strip steak
½ tsp fajita seasoning
2 tbsp corn

DIRECTIONS

Preheat your Air Fryer to 200°C. Combine the olive oil, onion, and salt in a bowl. Add the mushrooms and toss to coat. Spread in the frying basket. Sprinkle steak with salt, fajita seasoning, and black pepper.

Place steak on top of the mushroom mixture and Air Fry for 9 minutes, flipping steak once. Let rest on a cutting board for 5 minutes before cutting in half. Divide steak, mushrooms, corn, and onions between 2 plates and serve. Enjoy!

Red Pepper and Mozzarella Steak Subs

Serves: 2 | Total Time: 30 minutes

INGREDIENTS

1 hoagie bun baguette, halved
200g flank steak, sliced
½ white onion, sliced

½ red pepper, sliced
2 mozzarella cheese slices

DIRECTIONS

Preheat your Air Fryer to 160°C. Place the flank steak slices, onion, and red pepper on one side of the frying basket. Add the hoagie bun halves, crusty side up, to the other half of the air fryer. Bake for 10 minutes. Flip the hoagie buns. Cover both sides with one slice of mozzarella cheese. Gently stir the steak, onions, and peppers. Cook for 6 more minutes until the cheese is melted and the steak is juicy and crispy outside.

Remove the cheesy hoagie halves to a serving plate. Cover one side with the steak, and top with the onions and peppers. Close with the other cheesy hoagie half, slice into two pieces, and enjoy!

Greek Stuffed Peppers

Serves 6 | Total Time: 25 minutes

INGREDIENTS

6 small green peppers, halved lengthwise
6 diced Kalamata olives
3 tbsp olive oil

200g minced pork
30g feta cheese
75g Greek yogurt

DIRECTIONS

Warm 2 tbsp of olive oil in a skillet over medium heat. Stir in minced pork and cook for 6 minutes until no longer pink. Preheat your Air Fryer to 175°C. Mix the cooked pork, olives, and feta in a bowl.

Divide the mixture between the peppers. Place them in the frying basket and Air Fry for 10-12 minutes. Mix the Greek yogurt with the remaining olive oil in a small bowl. Serve with the peppers.

T-Bone Steak

Serves 2 | Total Time: 20 minutes

INGREDIENTS

2 tbsp butter, softened
¼ tsp lemon juice
2 cloves garlic, minced

1 T-bone steak
Salt and pepper to taste
¼ tsp onion powder

DIRECTIONS

In a small bowl, whisk butter, lemon juice, onion powder, and garlic. Transfer the mixture to a parchment paper. Roll into a log and spin ends to tighten. Let chill in the fridge for 2 hours. Remove the steak from the refrigerator 30 minutes before cooking. Season.

Preheat your Air Fryer to 200°C. Add the steak to the greased frying basket and Air Fry for 10 minutes, flipping once. Transfer the steak to a cutting board and let it sit for 5 minutes. Cut the butter mixture into slices and top the steak. Let the butter melt over before serving. Enjoy!

Lemon Skirt Steak

Serves 2 | Total Time: 20 minutes

INGREDIENTS

200 ml double cream
3 tbsp horseradish sauce
1 lemon, zested

350g skirt steak, halved
2 tbsp olive oil
Salt and pepper to taste

DIRECTIONS

Mix the double cream, horseradish sauce, and lemon zest in a small bowl. Let chill in the fridge.

Preheat your Air Fryer to 200°C. Brush steak halves with olive oil and sprinkle with salt and pepper. Place steaks in the frying basket and Air Fry for 10 minutes or until you reach your desired doneness, flipping once. Let sit for 5 minutes. Use a sharp knife to slice the grain into thin slices. Arrange on two plates. Drizzle the horseradish sauce over. Serve and enjoy!

Quick Sirloin Strips

Serves: 2 | Total Time: 25 minutes

INGREDIENTS

200g top sirloin strips
120g breadcrumbs
½ tsp garlic powder

½ tsp steak seasoning
2 eggs, beaten
Salt and pepper to taste

DIRECTIONS

Preheat your Air Fryer to 180°C. Put the breadcrumbs, garlic powder, steak seasoning, salt, and pepper in a bowl and stir to combine. Add in the sirloin steak strips and toss to coat all sides.

Dip into the beaten eggs, then dip again into the dry ingredients. Lay the coated steak pieces on the greased frying basket in an even layer. Air Fry for 16-18 minutes, turning once. Serve and enjoy!

Fried Beef Steaks

Serves: 4 | Total Time: 30 minutes

INGREDIENTS

Salt to taste
4 beef cube steaks
75 ml milk
120g flour

1 egg
120g bread crumbs
2 tbsp olive oil

DIRECTIONS

Preheat your Air Fryer to 180°C. Place the cube steaks in a zipper-sealed bag or between two sheets of cling wrap. Gently pound the steaks until they are slightly thinner. Set aside.

Mix the milk, flour, salt, and egg in a bowl until just combined. In a separate bowl, mix the crumbs and olive oil. Dip the steaks into the buttermilk batter, shake off the excess.

Next, dip the steaks in the bread crumbs, patting the crumbs on both sides. Air Fry the steaks until the crust is crispy and brown, 12-16 minutes. Serve warm.

Thyme Rib Eye Steak Bites

Serves: 4 | Total Time: 20 minutes

INGREDIENTS

500g rib eye steak, cubed
2 garlic cloves, minced
2 tbsp olive oil
1 tbsp thyme, chopped

1 tsp ground fennel seeds
Salt and pepper to taste
1 onion, thinly sliced

DIRECTIONS

Preheat your Air Fryer to 190°C. Place the steak, garlic, olive oil, thyme, fennel seeds, salt, pepper, and onion in a bowl. Mix until all of the beef and onion are well coated. Put the seasoned steak mixture into the frying basket. Roast for 10 minutes, stirring once. Let sit for 5 minutes. Serve.

Beef and Barley Stuffed Peppers

Serves: 4 | Total Time: 30 minutes

INGREDIENTS

4 peppers, tops removed
1 onion, chopped
2 tsp olive oil

2 tomatoes, chopped
100g cooked barley
150g pulled cooked roast beef

DIRECTIONS

Preheat your Air Fryer to 200°C. Cut the tops of the peppers, then remove the stems. Put the onion, olive oil, tomatoes, barley, and cooked beef in a bowl and stir to combine.

Spoon the veggie mix into the cleaned peppers and put them in the frying basket. Bake for 12-16 minutes or until the peppers are tender. Serve warm.

Beef and Veggie Skewers

Serves: 4 | Total Time: 25 minutes

INGREDIENTS

2 tbsp balsamic vinegar
2 tsp olive oil
Salt and pepper to taste
400g round steak, cubed

1 red pepper, sliced
1 yellow pepper, sliced
100g cherry tomatoes

DIRECTIONS

Preheat your Air Fryer to 195°C. Put the balsamic vinegar, olive oil, salt, and black pepper in a bowl and stir. Toss the steak in and allow to marinate for 10 minutes. Poke 8 metal skewers through the beef, peppers, and cherry tomatoes, alternating ingredients as you go.

Place the skewers in the air fryer and Air Fry for 5-7 minutes, turning once until the beef is golden and cooked through and the veggies are tender. Serve.

Beef Koftas

Serves: 6 | Total Time: 30 minutes

INGREDIENTS

1 medium onion, minced
2 garlic cloves, minced
1 tsp olive oil

1 bread slice, crumbled
3 tbsp milk
500g minced beef

DIRECTIONS

Preheat your Air Fryer to 190°C. Toss the onion, garlic, and olive oil in a baking pan, place it in the air fryer, and Air Fry for 2-4 minutes. The veggies should be crispy but tender.

Transfer the veggies to a bowl and add in the breadcrumbs, milk, thyme, and sage, then toss gently to combine. Add in the minced beef and mix with your hands. Mold the mixture into 12 koftas.

Put them in the frying basket and Air Fry for 12-16 minutes or until the meatballs are browned on all sides. Serve and enjoy!

Saturday Night Cheeseburgers

Serves: 4 | Total Time: 20 minutes

INGREDIENTS

500g minced beef
1 tsp Worcestershire sauce
1 tbsp allspice

Salt and pepper to taste
4 cheddar cheese slices
4 buns

DIRECTIONS

Preheat your Air Fryer to 180°C. Combine beef, Worcestershire sauce, allspice, salt, and pepper in a large bowl. Divide into 4 equal portions and shape into patties.

Place the burgers in the greased frying basket and Air Fry for 8 minutes. Flip and cook for another 3-4 minutes. Top each burger with cheddar cheese and cook for another minute until the cheese melts. Transfer to a bun and serve.

Beef Meatballs with Cheese

Serves: 4 | Total Time: 30 minutes

INGREDIENTS

3 tbsp buttermilk
40g bread crumbs
1 egg

Salt and pepper to taste
500g minced beef
20 Swiss cheese cubes

DIRECTIONS

Preheat your Air Fryer to 195°C. Mix buttermilk, crumbs, egg, salt, and pepper in a bowl. Using your hands, mix in minced beef until just combined. Shape into 20 balls.

Take one meatball and shape it around a Swiss cheese cube. Repeat this for the remaining meatballs. Lightly spray the meatballs with oil and place them into the frying basket.

Bake the meatballs for 10-13 minutes, turning once until they are cooked through. Serve and enjoy!

Mexican Beef Steaks

Serves: 4 | Total Time: 30 minutes

INGREDIENTS

1 chipotle pepper in adobo sauce, minced
500g skirt steak
¼ tsp fajita seasoning

Salt and pepper to taste

DIRECTIONS

Cut the steak into 4 equal pieces, then place them on a plate. Mix together chipotle pepper, adobo sauce, salt, pepper, and fajita seasoning in a bowl. Spread the mixture on both sides of the steak.

Preheat your Air Fryer to 195°C. Place the steaks in the frying basket and Bake for 5-7 minutes on each side for well-done meat. Allow the steaks to rest for 5 more minutes. To serve, slice against the grain.

BBQ Back Ribs

Serves: 4 | Total Time: 30 minutes

INGREDIENTS

2 tbsp brown sugar
Salt and pepper to taste
1 tsp garlic powder

½ tsp smoked paprika
700g baby back ribs
2 tbsp barbecue sauce

DIRECTIONS

Preheat your Air Fryer to 190°C. Combine the brown sugar, salt, pepper, garlic powder, and smoked paprika in a bowl and mix. Pour into a small glass jar.

Brush the ribs with barbecue sauce and sprinkle 1 tbsp of the seasoning mix. Rub the seasoning all over the meat. Set the ribs in the greased frying basket. Bake for 16-18 minutes until nicely browned, flipping them once. Serve hot!

Salsa Verde Tender Steak

Serves 4 | Total Time: 20 minutes + marinating time

INGREDIENTS

1 (1-kg) flank steak, halved
250g salsa verde

½ tsp black pepper

DIRECTIONS

Toss steak and about 200g of salsa verde in a bowl and refrigerate covered for 2 hours. Preheat your Air Fryer to 200°C. Add steaks to the lightly greased frying basket and Air Fry for 10-12 minutes or until you reach your desired doneness, flipping once. Let sit for 5 minutes.

Cut against the grain into thin slices and divide among four plates. Spoon over the remaining salsa verde and serve sprinkled with pepper.

Roast Beef Risotto with Parmesan

Serves: 4 | Total Time: 30 minutes

INGREDIENTS

½ chopped cooked roast beef
3 tbsp grated Parmesan cheese
2 tsp olive oil

1 shallot, finely chopped
3 garlic cloves, minced
120g short-grain rice

DIRECTIONS

Preheat your Air Fryer to 195°C. Add olive oil, shallot, and garlic to a baking pan and stir to combine. Air Fry for 2 minutes or until the vegetables are crisp-tender.

Remove from the air fryer and stir in the rice, 300 ml of water, and roast beef. Put the cooking pan back into the fryer. Bake for 18-22 minutes, stirring once until the rice is al dente. Sprinkle with Parmesan cheese and serve.

Cumin Beef Sliders

Serves 4 | Total Time: 25 minutes

INGREDIENTS

500g minced beef
¼ tsp cumin
¼ tsp mustard powder

40g grated yellow onion
½ tsp smoked paprika
Salt and pepper to taste

DIRECTIONS

Preheat your Air Fryer to 175°C. Combine the minced beef, cumin, mustard, onion, paprika, salt, and black pepper in a bowl. Form the mixture into 8 patties and make a slight indentation in the middle. Place beef patties in the greased frying basket and Air Fry for 8-10 minutes, flipping once. Serve.

Herby Jamaican Rib Eye Steak

Serves: 2 | Total Time: 15 minutes

INGREDIENTS

2 tsp Jamaican Jerk seasoning
350g Ribeye steak
2 thin butter slices

1 tsp chopped parsley
½ tsp fresh rosemary

DIRECTIONS

Preheat your Air Fryer to 200°C. Sprinkle Ribeye with Jamaican seasoning and rosemary on both sides. Place it in the basket and Bake for 10 minutes, turning once. Remove it to a cutting board and top with butter halves. Let rest for 5 minutes and scatter with parsley. Serve immediately.

Buttered Filet Mignon

Serves 2 | Total Time: 30 minutes

INGREDIENTS

2 filet mignon steaks
¼ tsp garlic powder

Salt and pepper to taste
1 tbsp butter, melted

DIRECTIONS

Preheat your Air Fryer to 185°C. Sprinkle the steaks with garlic powder, salt, and pepper. Place them in the greased frying basket and Air Fry for 12 minutes to yield a medium-rare steak, turning twice. Transfer steaks to a cutting board, brush them with butter, and let rest for 5 minutes before serving.

Holiday Ribeye Bites with Mushrooms

Serves: 4 | Total Time: 30 minutes

INGREDIENTS

600g boneless rib-eye or sirloin steak, cubed
250g button mushrooms, halved
4 tbsp olive oil
1 onion, chopped

2 garlic cloves, minced
Salt and pepper to taste
1 tsp dried parsley

DIRECTIONS

Preheat your Air Fryer to 200°C. Combine the rapeseed oil, onion, mushrooms, garlic, steak cubes, salt, pepper, and parsley in a baking pan. Put it in the frying basket and Bake for 12-15 minutes, stirring once or twice to ensure an even cooking, and until golden brown. The veggies should be tender. Serve hot.

Chilli Steak with Fried Eggs

Serves: 1 | Total Time: 25 minutes

INGREDIENTS

2 tsp olive oil
1 garlic clove, minced
240g sirloin steak
½ tsp chilli powder

Salt and black pepper to taste
2 eggs
2 dill pickles, sliced

DIRECTIONS

Preheat your Air Fryer to 200°C. Combine olive oil, garlic, chilli, salt, and pepper in a small bowl. Rub the spice mixture on the sirloin steak. Transfer the steak to the frying basket. Cook it for 7-10 minutes, flipping once. Remove the steak to a plate and cover loosely with foil. Allow it to rest.

Crack the eggs into a greased ramekin. Season with salt and pepper. Bake for 4-5 minutes until the egg whites are cooked and set. Remove the foil from the steak. Top with fried eggs and sliced pickles.

Paprika Ribeye Steak

Serves: 2 | Total Time: 25 minutes

INGREDIENTS

500g ribeye steak
Salt and pepper to taste
1 tbsp butter

1 tsp paprika
2 garlic cloves, minced
1 tbsp chopped mint

DIRECTIONS

Preheat your Air Fryer to 200°C. Sprinkle salt and pepper on the ribeye. Transfer it to the greased frying basket. Top with butter, paprika, and garlic. Bake for 12-14 minutes, flipping once. Allow resting for 5 minutes before slicing. Serve sprinkled with mint, and enjoy!

Provençal Ribeye Steak

Serves: 4 | Total Time: 25 minutes

INGREDIENTS

4 (320g each) ribeye steaks
1 tbsp herbs de Provence

Salt and pepper to taste

DIRECTIONS

Preheat your Air Fryer to 180°C. Season the steaks with herbs, salt, and pepper. Place them in the greased frying basket and cook for 8-12 minutes, flipping once. Use a thermometer to check for doneness and adjust time as needed. Let the steak rest for a few minutes and serve.

Easter Lamb Chops

Serves: 4 | Total Time: 30 minutes

INGREDIENTS

8 lamb chops

2 tsp olive oil

1 tsp ground coriander

1 lemon, zested

½ tsp za'atar seasoning

2 garlic cloves, minced

Salt and pepper to taste

DIRECTIONS

Place the couscous in a bowl and cover with 1 ½ cups of salted boiling water. Let sit until the water is absorbed. Preheat your Air Fryer to 195°C. Coat the lamb chops with olive oil. Mix the mint, coriander, lemon zest, za'atar, garlic, salt, and pepper in a bowl. Rub the seasoning onto the chops.

Place them in the greased frying basket and Air Fry for 14-16 minutes, flipping once. Let the lamb chops rest for a few minutes. Serve.

Tandoori Lamb Samosas

Serves: 2 | Total Time: 20 minutes

INGREDIENTS

200g minced lamb, sautéed

50g spinach, torn

½ onion, minced

1 tsp tandoori masala

Salt and pepper to taste

3 puff dough sheets

DIRECTIONS

Preheat your Air Fryer to 180°C. Put the minced lamb, tandoori masala, salt, and pepper in a bowl and stir to combine. Add in the spinach and onion and stir until the ingredients are evenly blended. Divide the mixture into three equal segments.

Lay the pastry dough sheets out on a lightly floured surface. Fill each sheet of dough with one of the three portions of lamb mix, then fold the pastry into a triangle, sealing the edges with a bit of water. Transfer the samosas to the greased frying basket and Air Fry for 12 minutes, flipping once until the samosas are crispy and flaky. Remove and leave to cool for 5 minutes. Serve.

Spicy Lamb Kebab

Serves: 2 | Total Time: 25 minutes

INGREDIENTS

3 lamb chops

120g breadcrumbs

2 eggs, beaten

Salt and pepper to taste

½ tbsp thyme

½ tbsp mint, chopped

DIRECTIONS

Preheat your Air Fryer to 160°C. Mix the breadcrumbs, thyme, mint, salt, and pepper in a bowl. Dip the lamb chops in the beaten eggs, then coat with the crumb mixture. Air Fry for 14-16 minutes, turning once. Serve and enjoy!

VEGETABLES AND SIDES

Hasselback Potatoes

Serves: 4 | Total Time: 45 minutes

INGREDIENTS

500g fingerling potatoes
1 tbsp olive oil
1 tbsp butter

1 tsp dried sage
Salt and pepper to taste

DIRECTIONS

Preheat your Air Fryer to 200°C. Rinse the potatoes dry, then set them on a work surface and put two chopsticks lengthwise on either side of each so you won't cut all the way through.

Make vertical, crosswise cuts in the potato, about 0.5 cm apart. Repeat with the remaining potatoes. Combine the olive oil and butter in a bowl and microwave for 30 seconds or until melted.

Stir in the sage, salt, and pepper. Put the potatoes in a large bowl and drizzle with the olive oil. Toss to coat, then put the potatoes in the fryer and Air Fry for 22-27 minutes, rearranging them after 10-12 minutes. Cook until the potatoes are tender.

Carrot and Parsnip Chips

Serves: 4 | Total Time: 40 minutes

INGREDIENTS

2 tbsp butter
2 tsp smoked paprika
1 tsp dried dill

Salt and pepper to taste
2 carrots, cut into rounds
1 parsnip, cut into rounds

DIRECTIONS

Preheat your Air Fryer to 190°C. Combine the butter, paprika, dried dill, salt, and pepper in a small pan over low heat until the butter melts. Put the carrots and parsnip in the frying basket, top with the butter mix, and toss. Air Fry for 20-25 minutes or until the veggies are tender and golden around the edges.

Herby Potatoes

Serves: 4 | Total Time: 30 minutes

INGREDIENTS

2 red potatoes, peeled and cubed
2 tbsp olive oil
1 tsp dried sage

½ tsp dried thyme
½ tsp salt
2 tbsp grated Parmesan cheese

DIRECTIONS

Preheat your Air Fryer to 180°C. Coat the red potatoes with olive oil, sage, thyme, and salt in a bowl. Pour the potatoes into the air frying basket and Roast for 10 minutes. Stir the potatoes and sprinkle the Parmesan cheese over the top. Continue roasting for 8 more minutes. Serve hot.

Spicy Brussels Sprouts

Serves: 4 | Total Time: 35 minutes

INGREDIENTS

500g Brussels sprouts, halved
1 tbsp olive oil
1 tbsp lemon juice
½ tsp salt

4 garlic cloves, sliced
2 tbsp parsley, chopped
½ tsp red chilli flakes

DIRECTIONS

Preheat your Air Fryer to 190°C. Combine the olive oil, lemon juice, and salt in a bowl and mix well. Add the Brussels sprouts and toss to coat. Put the Brussels sprouts in the frying basket.

Air Fry for 15-20 minutes, shaking the basket once, until golden and crisp. Sprinkle with garlic slices, parsley, and chilli flakes. Toss and cook for 2-4 minutes more until the garlic browns slightly.

Paprika Fried Mushrooms

Serves: 4 | Total Time: 30 minutes

INGREDIENTS

120g panko bread crumbs
150g white mushrooms
120g plain flour

1 egg
½ tsp smoked paprika
Salt and pepper to taste

DIRECTIONS

Preheat your Air Fryer to 200°C. Put the flour on a plate. Beat the egg with salt and pepper in a shallow bowl. Mix the panko bread crumbs and smoked paprika on a separate plate. Cut the mushrooms through the stems into quarters. Dip the mushrooms in flour, the egg, and the panko mix.

Press to coat then put on a wire rack and set aside. Add the mushrooms to the frying basket and spray with cooking oil. Air Fry for 6-8 minutes, flipping them once until crisp. Serve warm.

Chilli Broccoli

Serves: 4 | Total Time: 25 minutes

INGREDIENTS

1 chipotle pepper in adobo sauce, minced
500g broccoli
2 tbsp chilli oil
1 tbsp adobo sauce

2 tsp chilli powder
Salt and pepper to taste

DIRECTIONS

Preheat your Air Fryer to 190°C. Rinse the broccoli, shake it dry, and cut it into about 5 cm wide florets. Mix the chilli oil, chipotle pepper, adobo sauce, chilli powder, salt, and pepper in a bowl.

Add the broccoli and toss to coat evenly. Put the broccoli in the frying basket and Air Fry for 13-18 minutes, shaking the basket halfway through until the broccoli is crispy.

Zesty Middle Eastern Pepper Medley

Serves: 4 | Total Time: 40 minutes

INGREDIENTS

1 red pepper
1 orange pepper
1 yellow pepper

2 tsp Za'atar seasoning
1 tbsp lemon zest
½ tsp salt

DIRECTIONS

Preheat your Air Fryer to 185°C. Pierce the peppers with a fork a few times. Put them in the greased frying basket and Air Fry for 12-15 minutes, shaking once until slightly charred. Remove them to a small and let them sit covered for 10 minutes to steam. Slice the pepper and sprinkle with Za'atar seasoning, lemon zest, and salt. Serve and enjoy!

Honey Pumpkin Rounds

Serves: 4 | Total Time: 35 minutes

INGREDIENTS

1 (1-kg) pumpkin
1 tbsp honey
1 tbsp melted butter

¼ tsp cardamom
¼ tsp sea salt

DIRECTIONS

Preheat your Air Fryer to 185°C. Cut the pumpkin in half lengthwise and remove the seeds. Slice each half crosswise into 2.5-cm-wide half-circles, then cut each half-circle in half again to make quarter rounds. Combine the honey, butter, cardamom, and salt in a bowl and mix well.

Toss the pumpkin in the mixture until coated, then put it into the frying basket. Bake for 15-20 minutes, shaking once during cooking, until the edges start to brown and the squash is tender.

Savoury Truffle Vegetable Croquettes

Serves: 4 | Total Time: 40 minutes

INGREDIENTS

2 cooked potatoes, mashed
1 cooked carrot, mashed
1 tbsp onion, minced
2 eggs, beaten

2 tbsp olive oil
1 tbsp truffle oil
½ tbsp flour
Salt and pepper to taste

DIRECTIONS

Preheat your Air Fryer to 175°C. Sift the flour, salt, and pepper in a bowl and stir to combine. Add the potatoes, carrot, onion, olive oil, and truffle oil to a separate bowl and mix well. Shape the potato mixture into small bite-sized patties.

Dip the potato patties into the beaten eggs, coating thoroughly, then roll in the flour mixture to cover all sides. Arrange the croquettes in the greased frying basket and Air Fry for 14-16 minutes. Halfway through cooking, shake the basket. The croquettes should be crispy and golden. Serve hot and enjoy!

Breaded Artichoke Hearts

Serves: 2 | Total Time: 25 minutes

INGREDIENTS

450g tinned artichoke hearts in water, drained
1 egg
30g bread crumbs
¼ tsp salt

¼ tsp hot paprika
½ lemon

DIRECTIONS

Preheat your Air Fryer to 190°C. Whisk together the egg and 1 tbsp of water until frothy. Mix the bread crumbs, salt, and hot paprika separately.

Dip the artichoke hearts into the egg mixture, then coat in the breadcrumb mixture. Put the artichoke hearts in a single layer in the frying basket. Air Fry for 15 minutes. Remove the artichokes from the air fryer and squeeze fresh lemon juice over the top. Serve.

Green Vegetable Bake

Serves: 4 | Total Time: 15 minutes

INGREDIENTS

150g asparagus, chopped
250g broccoli florets
1 tbsp olive oil
1 tbsp lemon juice

150g green peas
2 tbsp honey mustard
Salt and pepper to taste

DIRECTIONS

Preheat your Air Fryer to 180°C. Add asparagus and broccoli to the frying basket. Drizzle with olive oil and lemon juice and toss. Bake for 6 minutes. Remove the basket and add peas.

Steam for another 3 minutes or until the vegetables are hot and tender. Pour the vegetables into a serving dish. Drizzle with honey mustard and season with salt and pepper. Toss and serve warm.

Sesame Baby Carrots

Serves: 4 | Total Time: 25 minutes

INGREDIENTS

500g baby carrots
1 tbsp sesame oil
Salt to taste

1 tsp smoked paprika
3 tbsp sesame seeds
1 tbsp green onions

DIRECTIONS

Preheat your Air Fryer to 190°C. In a bowl, add baby carrots, sesame oil, salt, and smoked paprika. Toss to coat. Transfer the carrots to the frying basket. Roast for about 4 minutes.

Shake the basket and continue roasting for another 4 minutes or until the garlic and carrots are slightly brown. Pour into a serving bowl and top with sesame seeds and green onions. Enjoy!

Gruyère Broccoli Au Gratin

Serves: 2 | Total Time: 25 minutes

INGREDIENTS

300g broccoli florets, chopped
7 tbsp grated Gruyère cheese
½ tbsp olive oil
1 tbsp flour

40 ml milk
Salt and black pepper
2 tbsp panko bread crumbs

DIRECTIONS

Preheat your Air Fryer to 180°C. Whisk the olive oil, flour, milk, salt, and pepper in a bowl. Incorporate broccoli, Gruyere cheese, and panko bread crumbs until well combined. Pour in a greased baking dish.

Put the baking dish into the frying basket. Bake until the broccoli is crisp-tender and the top is golden, or about 12-15 minutes. Serve warm.

Brussels Sprouts with Guanciale

Serves: 4 | Total Time: 50 minutes

INGREDIENTS

3 guanciale slices, halved
500g Brussels sprouts, halved
2 tbsp olive oil

¼ tsp salt
¼ tsp dried thyme

DIRECTIONS

Preheat your Air Fryer to 175°C. Lay the guanciale in the air fryer basket and Air Fry it until crispy, about 10 minutes. Remove and drain on a paper towel. Give the guanciale a rough chop and set aside.

Coat Brussels sprouts with olive oil in a large bowl. Add salt and thyme, then toss. Place the sprouts in the frying basket. Air Fry for about 12-15 minutes, shaking the basket once until the sprouts are golden and tender. Top with guanciale and serve.

Cheesy Cauliflower Pie with Olives

Serves: 4 | Total Time: 40 minutes

INGREDIENTS

60g cooked cauliflower, chopped
60g shredded cheddar
1 pie crust

2 eggs
6 black olives, chopped
Salt and pepper to taste

DIRECTIONS

Preheat your Air Fryer to 180°C. Grease and line a tart tin with the pie crust. Trim the edges and prick lightly with a fork. Whisk the eggs in a bowl until fluffy. Add cauliflower, salt, pepper, black olives, and half the cheese; stir to combine.

Carefully spoon the mixture into the pie crust and spread it level. Bake in the air fryer for 15 minutes. Slide the basket out and sprinkle the rest of the cheese on top. Cook for another 5 minutes until golden on the top and cooked through. Leave to cool before serving.

Rosemary Purple Potatoes

Serves: 4 | Total Time: 25 minutes

INGREDIENTS

500g purple potatoes, scrubbed and halved

1 tbsp olive oil

1 tsp Dijon mustard

2 cloves garlic, minced

Salt and pepper to taste

2 tbsp butter, melted

1 tsp fresh rosemary

DIRECTIONS

Preheat your Air Fryer to 175°C. Mix the olive oil, mustard, garlic, salt, pepper, and rosemary in a bowl. Set aside. Toss the potatoes, salt, pepper, and butter in a bowl, place the potatoes in the frying basket.

Roast for 18-20 minutes, tossing once. Transfer them into a bowl. Drizzle potatoes with the dressing and toss to coat. Serve.

Italian Breaded Aubergine Rounds

Serves: 4 | Total Time: 30 minutes

INGREDIENTS

1 aubergine, sliced into rounds

1 egg

60g bread crumbs

½ tsp Italian seasoning

½ tsp salt

½ tsp paprika

1 tbsp olive oil

DIRECTIONS

Preheat your Air Fryer to 180°C. Whisk the egg and 1 tbsp of water in a bowl until frothy. Mix the bread crumbs, Italian seasoning, salt, and paprika separately.

Dip the aubergine slices into the egg mixture, then coat them with the breadcrumb mixture. Put the slices in a single layer in the frying basket. Drizzle with olive oil. Air Fry for 23-25 minutes, turning once. Serve warm.

Creamy Cauliflower and Rutabaga Mash

Serves 4 | Total Time: 25 minutes

INGREDIENTS

1 head cauliflower, cut into florets

1 rutabaga, diced

4 tbsp butter, softened

Salt and pepper to taste

60g cream cheese, softened

75 ml milk

DIRECTIONS

Preheat your Air Fryer to 175°C. Combine cauliflower, rutabaga, 2 tbsp of butter, and salt to taste in a bowl. Add the vegetable mixture to the frying basket of the Air Fryer.

Air Fry for 15 minutes, tossing once halfway through. Allow the vegetables to cool slightly, then transfer them to a blender. Add the remaining butter, salt, black pepper, cream cheese, and milk. Blend until smooth. Serve immediately

Italian Arancini

Serves: 4 | Total Time: 20 minutes

INGREDIENTS

250g cooked rice

1 egg

3 tbsp all-purpose flour

½ cup finely grated carrots

¼ cup grated Parmesan cheese

2 tsp olive oil

DIRECTIONS

Preheat your Air Fryer to 190°C. In a bowl, mix together the cooked rice, egg, and all-purpose flour until well combined. Add in the grated carrots and Parmesan cheese, and mix again until evenly distributed.

Shape the mixture into 8 evenly sized patties. Brush each one with olive oil on both sides. Place the cakes in the frying basket of the Air Fryer. Air Fry for 8-10 minutes, flipping once halfway through, or until the fritters are golden and crispy on the outside. Serve and enjoy!

Potato, Aubergine and Onion Casserole

Serves: 4 | Total Time: 30 minutes

INGREDIENTS

1 Yukon Gold potato, sliced

1 aubergine, sliced

30g minced onions

120 ml milk

2 tbsp cornflour

Salt and pepper to taste

DIRECTIONS

Preheat your Air Fryer to 190°C. In a baking pan, layer the potato, aubergine, and onion. In a bowl, combine the milk, cornflour, salt, and pepper. Mix well, then pour this mixture over the layered vegetables.

Place the baking pan in the Air Fryer and bake for 15 minutes or until the casserole is golden on top and the vegetables are softened. Once cooked, remove from the Air Fryer and serve hot.

Courgette Fries with Pecorino Cheese

Serves 2 | Total Time: 30 minutes

INGREDIENTS

60g grated Pecorino cheese

1 courgette, cut into fries

1 tsp salt

1 egg

1 tbsp almond milk

60g almond flour

DIRECTIONS

Preheat your Air Fryer to 185°C. Distribute courgette fries evenly over a paper towel, sprinkle with salt, and let sit for 10 minutes to pull out moisture. Pat them dry with paper towels. In a bowl, beat egg and almond milk. In another bowl, combine almond flour and Pecorino cheese

Dip fries in egg mixture and then dredge them in flour mixture. Place courgette fries in the greased frying basket and Air Fry for 10 minutes, flipping once. Serve.

Effortless Cauliflower with Cheese

Serves 4 | Total Time: 25 minutes

INGREDIENTS

1 head cauliflower, cut into florets
3 tbsp butter, melted
2 tbsp grated asiago cheese

2 tsp dried sage
½ tsp garlic powder
¼ tsp salt

DIRECTIONS

Preheat your Air Fryer to 175°C. Mix all ingredients in a bowl. Add cauliflower mixture to the frying basket and Air Fry for 6 minutes, shaking once. Serve immediately.

Scrumptious Balsamic Beetroot Chips

Serves: 4 | Total Time: 40 minutes

INGREDIENTS

½ tsp balsamic vinegar
4 beetroots, peeled and sliced
1 garlic clove, minced

2 tbsp chopped mint
Salt and pepper to taste
3 tbsp olive oil

DIRECTIONS

Preheat your Air Fryer to 190°C. Coat all ingredients in a bowl except balsamic vinegar. Pour the beet mixture into the frying basket and Roast for 25-30 minutes, stirring once. Drizzle with vinegar. Enjoy!

Tarragon Courgette Bites

Serves: 4 | Total Time: 30 minutes

INGREDIENTS

1 tbsp grated Parmesan cheese
2 courgettes, sliced
120g breadcrumbs

2 eggs, beaten
Salt and pepper to taste
1 tsp dry tarragon

DIRECTIONS

Preheat your Air Fryer to 185°C. Place the breadcrumbs, Parmesan cheese, tarragon, salt, and pepper in a bowl and stir to combine. Dip the courgettes into the beaten eggs, then coat with Parmesan mixture.

Lay the courgette slices on the greased frying basket in an even layer. Air Fry for 14-16 minutes, shaking the basket several times during cooking. When ready, the courgette will be crispy and golden.

Cumin Sweet Potato Wedges

Serves: 4 | Total Time: 30 minutes

INGREDIENTS

2 peeled sweet potatoes, cubed
30g grated Parmesan cheese
1 tbsp olive oil

Salt and pepper to taste
½ tsp dried thyme
½ tsp ground cumin

DIRECTIONS

Preheat your Air Fryer to 165°C. Add sweet potato cubes to the frying basket, then drizzle with oil. Toss to gently coat. Season with salt, pepper, thyme, and cumin. Roast the potatoes for about 10 minutes.

Shake the basket and continue roasting for another 10 minutes. Shake the basket again, this time adding Parmesan cheese. Shake and return to the air fryer. Roast until the potatoes are tender, 4-6 minutes.

Orange-Glazed Broccoli Florets

Serves: 4 | Total Time: 20 minutes

INGREDIENTS

400g broccoli florets
2 tbsp olive oil
½ tsp salt

75 ml orange juice
1 tbsp honey
4-6 orange wedges

DIRECTIONS

Preheat your Air Fryer to 180°C. In a bowl, combine the broccoli florets, olive oil, salt, orange juice, and honey. Toss the broccoli in the liquid until well coated. Pour the broccoli mixture into the frying basket of the Air Fryer. Roast for 12 minutes, stirring once halfway through. Serve with orange wedges.

Chilli Asparagus

Serves: 4 | Total Time: 20 minutes

INGREDIENTS

500g asparagus, trimmed
2 tsp olive oil
3 garlic cloves, minced

2 tbsp balsamic vinegar
½ tsp dried thyme
½ red chilli, finely sliced

DIRECTIONS

Preheat your Air Fryer to 190°C. Put the asparagus and olive oil in a bowl and stir to coat, then put them in the frying basket. Toss some garlic over the asparagus and Roast for 4-8 minutes until crisp-tender. Spritz with balsamic vinegar and toss in some thyme leaves. Top with red chilli slices and serve.

Balsamic Cherry Tomatoes

Serves: 4 | Total Time: 20 minutes

INGREDIENTS

1 tbsp dried basil
1 tsp salt
2 tbsp balsamic vinegar

20 cherry tomatoes
1 tbsp olive oil

DIRECTIONS

Preheat your Air Fryer to 200°C. Poke each cherry tomato with a toothpick to prevent bursting. Put the tomatoes, balsamic vinegar, and olive oil on aluminum foil and sprinkle with basil and salt; toss.

Wrap the foil around the tomatoes, leaving air space in the packet, and seal loosely. Put the packet in the air fryer and Bake for 8-10 minutes or until the tomatoes are tender.

Sautéed Green Beans

Serves: 6 | Total Time: 15 minutes

INGREDIENTS

1 tbsp coriander, chopped
500g green beans, trimmed
½ red onion, sliced
2 tbsp olive oil

Salt and pepper to taste
1 tbsp grapefruit juice
6 lemon wedges

DIRECTIONS

Preheat your Air Fryer to 180°C. Coat the green beans, red onion, olive oil, salt, pepper, coriander, and grapefruit juice in a bowl. Pour the mixture into the air fryer and Bake for 5 minutes. Stir well and cook for 5 minutes more. Serve with lemon wedges. Enjoy!

Garlicky Asparagus and Cherry Tomatoes

Serves: 6 | Total Time: 20 minutes

INGREDIENTS

2 tbsp dill, chopped
200g cherry tomatoes
700g asparagus, trimmed

2 tbsp olive oil
3 garlic cloves, minced
½ tsp salt

DIRECTIONS

Preheat your Air Fryer to 190°C. Add all ingredients to a bowl, except for dill, and toss until the vegetables are well coated with the oil. Pour the vegetable mixture into the frying basket and Roast for 11-13 minutes, shaking once. Serve topped with fresh dill.

Thyme Pumpkin Wedges with Parmesan Cheese

Serves: 4 | Total Time: 35 minutes

INGREDIENTS

250g pumpkin, cubed
2 tbsp olive oil
Salt and pepper to taste

¼ tsp pumpkin pie spice
1 tbsp thyme
30g grated Parmesan cheese

DIRECTIONS

Preheat your Air Fryer to 180°C. Put the cubed pumpkin with olive oil, salt, pumpkin pie spice, black pepper, and thyme in a bowl and stir until the pumpkin is well coated. Pour this mixture into the frying basket and Roast for 18-20 minutes, stirring once. Sprinkle the pumpkin with grated Parmesan cheese.

Pancetta-Wrapped Asparagus

Serves: 4 | Total Time: 30 minutes

INGREDIENTS

20 asparagus trimmed
Salt and pepper to taste

4 pancetta slices
1 tbsp fresh sage, chopped

DIRECTIONS

Sprinkle the asparagus with fresh sage, salt, and pepper. Toss to coat. Make 4 bundles of 5 spears by wrapping the center of the bunch with one slice of pancetta.

Preheat your Air Fryer to 200°C. Put the bundles in the greased frying basket and Air Fry for 8-10 minutes or until the pancetta is brown and the asparagus starts to char on the edges. Serve immediately.

Pancetta and Artichoke Heart Sautée

Serves 4 | Total Time: 20 minutes

INGREDIENTS

500g artichoke hearts, halved
1 onion, cut into half-moons
4 pancetta slices, diced

1 garlic clove, minced

DIRECTIONS

Preheat your Air Fryer to 175°C. Add all ingredients, except garlic, to the frying basket and stir well. Air Fry for 8 minutes, tossing once. Mix in the garlic and cook for 1 more minute. Serve.

Cheesy Potatoes Dauphinoise

Serves: 4 | Total Time: 30 minutes

INGREDIENTS

60g grated cheddar cheese
3 peeled potatoes, sliced
75 ml milk

75 ml double cream
Salt and pepper to taste
1 tsp ground nutmeg

DIRECTIONS

Preheat your Air Fryer to 175°C. Place the milk, double cream, salt, pepper, and nutmeg in a bowl and mix well. Dip in the potato slices and arrange on a baking dish. Spoon the remaining mixture over the potatoes. Scatter the grated cheddar cheese on top. Place the baking dish in the air fryer and Bake for 20 minutes. Serve warm and enjoy!

Dilly Sesame Asparagus Spears

Serves 6 | Total Time: 15 minutes

INGREDIENTS

500g asparagus, trimmed
1 tbsp olive oil
¼ tsp salt

1 garlic clove, minced
2 tsp chopped dill
3 tbsp sesame seeds

DIRECTIONS

Preheat your Air Fryer to 200°C. Place the trimmed asparagus on the air frying basket. Drizzle the olive oil over the asparagus. Sprinkle with salt. Roast the asparagus in the air fryer for 9 minutes or until tender and lightly browned, tossing once. Transfer it to a serving dish. Top with garlic, sesame seeds, and dill. Serve immediately.

Chipotle Avocado Wedges

Serves 4 | Total Time: 15 minutes

INGREDIENTS

½ tsp smoked paprika
2 tsp olive oil
½ lime, juiced

8 peeled avocado wedges
1 tsp chipotle powder
¼ tsp salt

DIRECTIONS

Preheat your Air Fryer to 200°C. Drizzle the avocado wedges with olive oil and lime juice. In a bowl, combine chipotle powder, smoked paprika, and salt. Sprinkle over the avocado wedges. Place them in the frying basket and Air Fry for 7 minutes. Serve immediately.

Roasted Cherry Tomatoes

Serves: 2 | Total Time: 15 minutes

INGREDIENTS

10 cherry tomatoes, halved
1 tsp olive oil

Salt to taste
2 tsp balsamic vinegar

DIRECTIONS

Preheat your Air Fryer to 190°C. Combine all ingredients in a bowl. Arrange the cherry tomatoes on the frying basket and Bake for 8 minutes until the tomatoes are blistered, shaking once. Serve drizzled with balsamic vinegar.

Tahini Parsnips and Carrots

Serves 4 | Total Time: 20 minutes

INGREDIENTS

2 parsnips, cut into half-moons
2 tsp olive oil
½ tsp salt
1 carrot, cut into sticks

1 tbsp tahini
1 tbsp lemon juice
1 garlic clove, minced

DIRECTIONS

Preheat your Air Fryer to 190°C. Coat the parsnips and carrots with olive oil and salt. Place them in the frying basket and Air Fry for 10 minutes, tossing once. In a bowl, whisk tahini, lemon juice, 1 tsp of water, and garlic. Pour the sauce over the cooked veggies. Serve.

Hot Courgette Ribbons

Serves 4 | Total Time: 15 minutes

INGREDIENTS

2 courgettes
2 tsp butter, melted
¼ tsp garlic powder

¼ tsp chilli flakes
8 cherry tomatoes, halved
Salt and pepper to taste

DIRECTIONS

Preheat your Air Fryer to 140°C. Cut the courgettes into ribbons with a vegetable peeler. Mix them with butter, garlic, chilli flakes, salt, and pepper in a bowl. Transfer to the frying basket and Air Fry for 2 minutes. Toss and add the cherry tomatoes. Cook for another 2 minutes. Serve.

Pecorino Cheese Muffins

Serves 4 | Total Time: 25 minutes

INGREDIENTS

30g grated Pecorino cheese
120g flour
⅛ tsp salt

2 tsp baking powder
1 egg
30g Greek yogurt

DIRECTIONS

Preheat your Air Fryer to 175°C. In a bowl, combine the dry ingredients. Set aside. In another bowl, whisk the wet ingredients. Add the wet ingredients to the dry ingredients and mix until blended. Transfer the batter to 6 silicone muffin cups lightly greased with olive oil. Place muffin cups in the frying basket and Bake for 12 minutes. Serve right away.

Spinach Chips

Serves: 4 | Total Time: 20 minutes

INGREDIENTS

300g spinach
2 tbsp lemon juice
2 tbsp olive oil

Salt and pepper to taste
½ tsp garlic powder
½ tsp onion powder

DIRECTIONS

Preheat your Air Fryer to 175°C. Place the spinach in a bowl and drizzle with lemon juice and olive oil; massage with your hands. Scatter with salt, pepper, garlic, and onion and gently toss to coat. Arrange the leaves in a single layer and Bake for 3 minutes. Shake and Bake for another 1-3 minutes until brown. Let cool.

Parmesan Popcorn

Serves: 2 | Total Time: 15 minutes

INGREDIENTS

2 tsp grated Parmesan cheese
30g popcorn kernels

1 tbsp lemon juice
1 tsp garlic powder

DIRECTIONS

Preheat your Air Fryer to 200°C. Line the basket with aluminum foil. Put the popcorn kernels in a single layer and Grill for 6-8 minutes until they stop popping. Remove them to a bowl. Drizzle with lemon juice and toss until well coated. Sprinkle with garlic powder and Parmesan cheese. Drizzle with more lemon juice. Serve.

Gorgonzola Stuffed Mushrooms

Serves 2 | Total Time: 15 minutes

INGREDIENTS

2 tbsp diced white button mushroom stems
12 white button mushroom caps
30g Gorgonzola cheese, crumbled
1 tsp olive oil

1 green onion, chopped
2 tbsp bread crumbs

DIRECTIONS

Preheat your Air Fryer to 175°C. Rub around the top of each mushroom cap with olive oil. Mix the mushroom stems, green onion, and Gorgonzola cheese in a bowl.

Distribute and press the mixture into the cups of mushrooms, then sprinkle bread crumbs on top. Place stuffed mushrooms in the frying basket and Bake for 5-7 minutes. Serve right away.

Sweet Almonds

Serves: 2 | Total Time: 10 minutes

INGREDIENTS

250g almonds
2 tsp maple syrup

2 tbsp cacao powder

DIRECTIONS

Preheat your Air Fryer to 175°C. Distribute the almonds in a single layer in the frying basket and Bake for 3 minutes. Shake the basket and Bake for another 1 minute until golden brown.

Remove them to a bowl. Drizzle with maple syrup and toss. Sprinkle with cacao powder and toss until well coated. Let cool completely. Store in a container at room temperature for up to 2 weeks or in the fridge for up to a month.

Okra Chips

Serves: 2 | Total Time: 20 minutes

INGREDIENTS

2 eggs
40 ml whole milk
30g bread crumbs
30g cornmeal

Salt and pepper to taste
200g okra, sliced
1 tbsp olive oil

DIRECTIONS

Preheat your Air Fryer to 200°C. Beat the eggs and milk in a bowl. In another bowl, combine the remaining ingredients, except okra and olive oil.

Dip okra chips in the egg mixture, then dredge them in the breadcrumbs mixture. Place okra chips in the greased frying basket and Roast for 7 minutes, shake once and drizzle with olive oil. Serve.

Blistered Shishito Peppers

Serves 2 | Total Time: 15 minutes + marinating time

INGREDIENTS

200g shishito peppers
2 tsp olive oil
1 tsp white wine vinegar

2 garlic cloves, minced
Salt to taste
1 tsp parsley, chopped

DIRECTIONS

Preheat your Air Fryer to 190°C. Arrange the peppers on the greased frying basket and Air Fry for 8 minutes or until blistered and softened, turning the peppers once.

Whisk the oil, vinegar, salt, garlic, and parsley in a bowl. Stir in the blistered peppers and let them sit for 1 hour. Serve.

Cholula Brown Onion Rings

Serves: 4 | Total Time: 30 minutes

INGREDIENTS

1 large brown onion
60g chickpea flour
50 ml milk

2 tbsp Cholula hot sauce
100g bread crumbs

DIRECTIONS

Preheat your Air Fryer to 190°C. Cut 1cm off the top of the onion's root, then cut into 1cm thick rings. Set aside. Combine the chickpea flour, milk, and hot sauce in a bowl.

In another bowl, add breadcrumbs. Submerge each ring into the flour batter until well coated, then dip into the breadcrumbs and Air Fry for 14 minutes until crispy, turning once. Serve.

Sweet and Spicy Roasted Acorn Squash

Serves: 2 | Total Time: 45 minutes

INGREDIENTS

½ acorn squash half
1 tsp olive oil
2 tsp light brown sugar

1/8 tsp ground cinnamon
2 tbsp hot sauce
40 ml maple syrup

DIRECTIONS

Preheat your Air Fryer to 200°C. Slice off about 0.5 cm from the side of the squash half to sit flat like a bowl. In a bowl, combine all ingredients.

Brush over the top of the squash and pour any remaining mixture in the middle of the squash. Place squash in the frying basket and Roast for 35 minutes. Remove and cut it in half, then divide between 2 serving plates. Serve.

Baked Green Beans with Bacon

Serves 4 | Total Time: 15 minutes

INGREDIENTS

250g green beans, trimmed
1 tbsp butter, melted
Salt and pepper to taste

1 bacon slice, diced
1 garlic clove, minced
1 tbsp balsamic vinegar

DIRECTIONS

Preheat your Air Fryer to 190°C. Combine green beans, butter, salt, and pepper in a bowl. Put the bean mixture in the frying basket and Air Fry for 5 minutes. Stir in bacon and Air Fry for 4 more minutes. Mix in garlic and cook for 1 minute. Transfer it to a serving dish and drizzle with balsamic vinegar. Serve right away.

Prawn Pancake

Serves: 4 | Total Time: 15 minutes

INGREDIENTS

1 tbsp olive oil
3 eggs, beaten
60g plain flour
60ml milk

⅛ tsp salt
150g salsa
200g cooked prawns, minced

DIRECTIONS

Preheat your Air Fryer to 185°C. Mix the olive oil, eggs, flour, milk, and salt in a bowl until frothy. Pour the batter into a greased baking pan and place it in the air fryer. Bake for 15 minutes or until the pancake is puffed and golden. Flip the pancake onto a plate. Mix the salsa and prawns. Top the pancake with the mixture and serve.

Sage Blackened Prawns

Serves: 4 | Total Time: 15 minutes

INGREDIENTS

500g peeled prawns, deveined
1 tsp paprika
½ tsp dried sage

½ tsp red chilli flakes
½ lemon, juiced
Salt and pepper to taste

DIRECTIONS

Preheat your Air Fryer to 200°C. Add prawns, paprika, sage, red chilli flakes, lemon juice, salt, and pepper to a resealable bag. Seal and shake well. Place the prawns in the greased frying basket and Air Fry for 7-8 minutes, shaking the basket once until blackened. Let cool slightly and serve.

SWEETS

Honey Stuffed Figs with Cheese

Serves: 4 | Total Time: 15 minutes

INGREDIENTS

8 figs, stem off
60g cottage cheese
¼ tsp ground cinnamon

¼ tsp orange zest
2 tbsp honey
1 tbsp olive oil

DIRECTIONS

Preheat your Air Fryer to 180°C. Cut an "X" in the top of each fig 1/3 way through, leaving intact the base. Mix together the cottage cheese, cinnamon, orange zest, and 1 tbsp of honey in a bowl.

Spoon the cheese mixture into the cavity of each fig. Put the figs in a single layer in the frying basket. Drizzle the olive oil over the figs and Roast for 10 minutes. Drizzle with the remaining honey. Serve and enjoy!

Pecan and Ginger Apples

Serves: 4 | Total Time: 20 minutes

INGREDIENTS

2 cored Granny Smith apples, halved
30g rolled oats
2 tbsp honey
½ tsp ground ginger

2 tbsp chopped pecans
A pinch of salt
1 tbsp olive oil

DIRECTIONS

Preheat your Air Fryer to 190°C. Combine the oats, honey, ginger, pecans, salt, and olive oil in a bowl. Scoop a quarter of the oat mixture onto the top of each apple half. Put the apples in the frying basket and Roast for 12-15 minutes until the apples are fork-tender.

Cinnamon Bread Pudding

Serves: 4 | Total Time: 30 minutes

INGREDIENTS

4 bread slices
230 ml milk
30g sugar

2 eggs, beaten
½ tsp ground cinnamon

DIRECTIONS

Preheat your Air Fryer to 160°C. Slice bread into bite-size pieces. Set aside in a small cake pan. Mix the milk, sugar, eggs, and cinnamon in a bowl until well combined. Pour over the bread and toss to coat. Bake for 20 minutes until crispy and all liquid is absorbed. Slice into 4 pieces. Serve.

Lemon Spring Banana Rolls

Serves: 4 | Total Time: 20 minutes

INGREDIENTS

2 ripe bananas, halved crosswise
4 spring roll wrappers
120 ml molasses

30g peanut butter
1 tsp lemon zest

DIRECTIONS

Preheat your Air Fryer to 190°C. Place the roll wrappers on a flat surface with one corner facing up. Spread 1 tbsp of molasses on each, then 1 tbsp of peanut butter, and finally top with lemon zest and 1 banana half. For the wontons, fold the bottom over the banana, then fold the sides and roll up. Place them seam-side down and Roast for 10 minutes until golden brown and crispy.

Cinnamon Spanish Churros

Serves: 5 | Total Time: 35 minutes

INGREDIENTS

¼ tsp salt
2 tbsp vegetable oil
3 tbsp white sugar

130g plain flour
½ tsp ground cinnamon
2 tbsp castor sugar

DIRECTIONS

Add 1 cup of water, salt, 1 tbsp of oil, and 1 tbsp sugar to a pot over high heat. Bring to a boil. Remove from the heat and add flour. Stir with a wooden spoon until the flour is combined and a ball of dough forms. Cool for 5 minutes.

Put the dough ball in a plastic pastry bag with a star tip. Squeeze the dough to the tip and twist the top of the bag. Squeeze 10 strips of dough, about 13-cm long each, onto a workspace. Spray with cooking oil.

Preheat your Air Fryer to 180°C. Place the churros in the greased frying basket and Air Fry for 22-25 minutes, flipping once halfway through until golden. Meanwhile, heat the remaining vegetable oil in a small bowl. In another shallow bowl, mix the remaining 2 tbsp sugar and cinnamon. Roll the cooked churros in cinnamon sugar. Top with castor sugar and serve immediately.

Kiwi Brownies

Serves: 4 | Total Time: 30 minutes + chilling time

INGREDIENTS

1 peeled kiwi, mashed
200 ml maple syrup
2 eggs, beaten

60g plain flour
½ tsp baking powder

DIRECTIONS

Preheat your Air Fryer to 160°C. Mix the kiwi, maple syrup, and eggs in a bowl. Toss in flour and baking powder until smooth. Pour the batter into a small round cake pan and Bake for 20 minutes until a toothpick comes out clean. Allow to cool completely before slicing into 4 brownies. Serve and enjoy!

Nutmeg Caramelized Apples

Serves: 2 | Total Time: 25 minutes

INGREDIENTS

2 apples, sliced
1 ½ tsp brown sugar
¼ tsp cinnamon

¼ tsp nutmeg
¼ tsp salt
1 tsp lemon zest

DIRECTIONS

Preheat your Air Fryer to 190°C. Set the apples upright in a baking pan. Add 2 tbsp of water to the bottom to keep the apples moist.

Sprinkle the tops with sugar, lemon zest, cinnamon, and nutmeg. Lightly sprinkle the halves with salt and the tops with oil. Bake for 20 minutes or until the apples are tender and golden on top. Enjoy.

Chocolate Cupcakes

Serves: 2 | Total Time: 25 minutes + cooling time

INGREDIENTS

60g white sugar
320g flour
2 tsp baking powder
½ tsp salt

160 ml sunflower oil
1 egg
170g chocolate chips

DIRECTIONS

Preheat your Air Fryer to 175°C. Combine sugar, flour, baking powder, and salt in a bowl and stir to combine. Whisk the egg in a separate bowl. Pour in the sunflower oil and continue whisking until light and fluffy. Spoon the wet mixture into the dry ingredients and stir to combine.

Gently fold in the chocolate chips with a spatula. Divide the batter between cupcake cups and Bake in the air fryer for 12-15 minutes or until a toothpick comes out dry. Remove the cupcakes and let them cool. Serve.

Cinnamon Rolls

Serves: 4 | Total Time: 40 minutes

INGREDIENTS

500g pizza dough
40g dark brown sugar

¼ cup butter, softened
½ tsp ground cinnamon

DIRECTIONS

Preheat your Air Fryer to 180°C. Roll out the dough into a rectangle. Using a knife, spread the brown sugar and butter, covering all the edges, and sprinkle with cinnamon. Fold the long side of the dough into a log, then cut it into 8 equal pieces, avoiding compression. Place the rolls, spiral-side up, onto a parchment-lined sheet. Let rise for 20 minutes. Grease the rolls with cooking spray and Bake for 8 minutes until golden brown. Serve right away.

Printed in Great Britain
by Amazon